D1490955

Table of Contents

SECRET #7: MAKING PEACE, PRACTICING GRATITUDE, AND
CELEBRATING!

fine
f^{to}ab

7 Secrets
*of a Successful
Woman's Journey
Away from Depression,
Disordered Eating
& Self-Sabotage*

Lisa Lieberman-Wang

Kim Bonniksen, Editor, The Legend People

CONTACT LISA

To Book Lisa for Corporate Events
call 1-877-250-7275
For more information, go to
www.LisaLiebermanWang.com

For most current book alumnus promotions see www.finetofab.com

FIRST EDITON

Author: Lisa Lieberman-Wang

fine to fab
7 Secrets of a Successful Woman's Journey Away from Depression, Disordered Eating & Self-Sabotage

ISBN # 978-1481095365

This book is dedicated to you, my reader, for your desire to move forward and become a better you, to live a life of true fulfillment.

This book is also dedicated to the thousands of individuals around the world who have joined the never-ending journey of self-improvement. Your continuous dedication to improving yourself has inspired me to be a better me.

It is because of you that this book is possible. Empowering and inspiring others to share their unsaid and unheard truth is what makes us real and enables us to live an authentic life that is healthy, happy, and free.

I also dedicate this book to the most important lesson-givers in my lifetime – my Grandma Susan, my mother and my father.

Finally, this book is dedicated to my husband, Yardley, for teaching me how to believe in myself like no other. He has been my raving fan since the beginning and very much the reason this book is in your hands.

I love you, Handsome!

Foreword

The key to health is so easy, even the Caveman knew it. Here's what I mean...

When you (or, at least, when your cavemen ancestors) were confronted with a life-or-death issue like an attack by a fierce carnivore, you needed to immediately activate your fight-or-flight mechanism in order to save your life. That was a good thing and it worked. It worked to save your caveman life. However... it had negative side-effects, too. But these were not as significant as the fact that you survived the incident.

The problem is: life is different today than it was back then, but your physiology hasn't changed all that much and the fight or flight mechanism is now over-utilized because it really isn't needed much anymore, hence resulting in a physiological catastrophe.

What is the fight-or-flight mechanism? It is the release of degenerative hormones: Cortisol and Adrenaline. They spur you into action. They save your life. They put you in top performance. But, alas, they also create stress. These two hormones and the related stress they cause are believed to be the leading cause of the most serious diseases like cancer, shingles, heart ailments, eating disorders and many others.

If the release of these hormones was so good for your cavemen ancestors, then why is it not good for you now? The reason is that the issues which cause you worry and stress today are no longer life-threatening. They may include someone angry at you, a very long red light, a nasty email, etc. Though there is no danger involved in these incidents, the body still perceives these incidents as danger and triggers the fight-or-flight mechanisms. The unused hormones in your system are the cause of the degeneration.

These unused and mostly unneeded hormones accumulate in your system and are the beginnings of the degenerative diseases you fear. The cure of the most dreaded diseases like cancer can be traced back to curing the release of, and the consequential accumulation of, the Cortisol and Adrenaline hormones in your body. And, how is that done? The ultimate answer is: ...being calm; ...playing contemplative music; ...resting during the day; ...getting sufficient sleep; ...enjoying the occasional massage; ...meditating; ...having peaceful retreats in your day; ...smiling; ...taking deep breaths when you feel stress; ...soaking in hot baths and if you are one of the 24 million women, 65% of all women who suffer from an eating disorder, practicing the 7-step prescription to stop the self-sabotage from Lisa Lieberman-Wang.

So your "homework" is to take a nice relaxing break and laugh and learn with Lisa while she teaches you how to follow her path from f.i.n.e. (F*@%*d Up, Insecure, Neurotic & Emotional...fine) to F.A.B. (Fabulous, Awesome & Beautiful). Yes, your prescription is to learn to live a more peaceful and empowered life. Enjoy it... because you deserve to be FAB!

Raymond Aaron
NY Times Bestselling author of Chicken Soup
for the Parent's Soul

Introduction

My story of *fine......*

F*@%*d Up, Insecure, Neurotic and Emotional...*fine*

I thought I was terminally unique. *"What's wrong with me?", "No one understands me"* or *"My problems are worse than yours."* Have you ever felt that way? Well I did, like I was carrying the weight of the world on my shoulders, couldn't get out of my own way, was trying to do everything for everyone and they still weren't happy. Life was a battlefield of perfection seeking, to look, and to be a certain way, to please the world to qualify for love. To my readers... I'm sure this has never been your experience... you have never worried about someone else's opinion of you, you have never changed your outfit fifty times to make sure you didn't look fat, you have never felt alone and unloved. The truth is, if you have never felt that way, you are alone... the rest of us are a powerful, but disconnect army of intelligent, beautiful women who struggle every day to be good enough... which are you? Alone or with the rest of us?

These destructive beliefs almost killed me.

Like all of us, food played an important role in my life growing up. I grew up in a home where food meant love through many generations. My great grandparents, my grandparents and my parents all relied on food to communicate love. That was our bonding time. It made them happy to see us eat and we were happy to be eating. My Grandma Laura had the best candy and I used to leave with my pockets stuffed and an extra fistful every visit. In my childish attempt to experience more love, I was hoarding food like a squirrel from an early age. Grandma Susan loved food so much that the topic of the dinner conversation was usually what we would eat at our next meal.

Like most of us, some of my best memories centered on food, but now I realize that many of those patterns set me up for a lifetime of pain.

Much research has confirmed the psychological patterns of our creation of self-fulfilling prophecies... all so that we can prove ourselves right. You tell yourself so long that you're bad and you are not enough, that unconsciously you do what you need to do so that you're right. When we say, even in jest or self-deprecation, "I'm so fat," we end up making ourselves fat to prove ourselves right. No matter how skinny I was I always worried about being fat. I was always scared of the scale. It could be the best day I had and as soon as I got on the scale, if the number wasn't a good number it would ruin my entire day. It just totally destroyed me. See if this is familiar to you... I would move the scale around the room to see if I could get a better number to improve my day. The scale was like a bad fortune teller. It would tell me I was never good enough, skinny enough, bright enough, attractive enough or lovable enough. It reinforced all the negative feelings I already had and validated me and gave me more reasons to hate myself.

By the age of eighteen, I was almost dead.

Unfortunately, it took me thirteen years to figure it out. When my food denial manifested itself in stomach pain and ulcers, the doctors prescribed medication for the ulcers, then told me to go home and relax, and avoid stress. Ha!...great idea, but not likely for Ms. Overachiever, can't sit still, have to be the best. Naturally, the ulcers only got worse and before I knew it, I could no longer keep food in my stomach, let alone liquids. Everything was coming up, like a gag reflux that I had no control over. I lost 30lbs in 30 days and thought I had no control over what was happening to me and ended up being admitted through the emergency room, weighing in at an emaciated 95 pounds, with my potassium so dangerously low that I suffered what they called a "sudden heart attack" at the ripe old age of 18.

Though many would have been convinced to change after this, my penchant for self-destruction knew no limits. I wish I could end here with a happily ever after, but it was too soon. There was a lot of drama in the following years, as we all seem to find a home for that in our lives. Being an extremist, I seemed to let it take over my life. Five emergency hospitalizations, tons of therapy, self-help programs, support groups, I was looking for the answer and only learning more ways to hurt myself. In a quest to feel whole, I was so smart that I almost missed the answers because they were so easy. In all the turmoil, I felt alone, lost, angry, sad, depressed, isolated, misunderstood, shame, unworthy, broken, not good enough, resentful, self-loathing, never feeling skinny enough and trying to fit into other people's models of what I should look like. After losing 30lbs in 30 days and becoming deathly ill I learned something in the hospital that changed my life. I discovered I had a gag reflex that enabled me to get rid of my food without having to put my fingers down my throat. This was the beginning of my real nightmare. I started the big lie. I found a way to stuff my feelings and not be found out, I could consume everything in sight then purge and no one would ever know. I found a way to avoid my mom's pain of suffering and ridicule. I can eat whatever I wanted and not get fat.

It all seemed to have happened so fast and it became a vicious cycle that I had no way of ending. I went through the next decade over the toilet bowl. I became obsessed. I found the answer, I can fill the void with food and then get rid of it all and purge making believe it never happened. More challenges started to arise that I didn't plan on. I was gaining weight. How could this be, I was getting rid of it all, or was I? I had to start color coding my food. Tracking the food that went in and making sure the same colors came out. I got really good at it. I was an anomaly, I was a skinny bulimic, most are 10-15lbs over weight but I perfected it. What a thing to perfect.

My binges started out small, I'd eat a little more to the point of full at a meal and then get rid of it and then they became bigger. I mean really big. Before I knew it I was compulsively overeating, binging and purging all the time. I was eating everything I could get my hands on. By this time my family threatened to lock the cabinets and the refrigerator. They never did it but I had to get smarter about it. I would go to the store to replace all that I had eaten so they wouldn't know I was still doing it. Then I would go out and buy food and make believe I was buying for the family and I would eat it all in the car before I ever got home and get rid of it in a public bathroom or on the side of the road. I felt like I was living in a fog. Over the years it got progressively worse. I used food for everything. If I did well it was there for the celebration and if I did poorly it was there for consolation.

I managed to graduate college with honors and partial scholarships, had an internship with IBM and taught dance at Arthur Murray while I spent the rest of my time binging and purging. I do not remember sleeping those years it is all a blur now to me.

Hospitalizations served as my warning signs that I had taken it too far and I needed to stop. They became my vacation. I can think of better vacations than a hospital these days. I didn't know how to stop; I needed to be rolled over by a tank to get my attention. I was either compulsively eating or working, there was no in between.

Thirty years ago they didn't know how to deal with eating disorders and they would address my malnutrition by getting my electrolytes back in sync, then send me off to a psych ward with seriously ill people and send me home after I gained a few pounds. It became a pattern that I mastered 5 times over.

The next solution to fix my problem was to send me for therapy. This presented another situation; my dad didn't believe in it and thought it was for crazy people. I am not sure that I agreed with dad, but I can say it was like having a scab and having someone rip it off you and send you out raw to heal only to come back the following week to open the wound again. I spent many years opening wounds that never really healed.

By the time I finished college and moved out my disease with myself was at an all-time high. I had started my own business and had people working for me. I was making more money than I could have ever imagined and I was binging and purging 18 times a day. I didn't have to sneak anymore or replace the food, worry about being found out, it was easy and dangerous. I ended up in the hospital again and this time I had an embarrassment I did not expect. I got audited because my accountant at the time didn't file a form properly. I was in the hospital and I called upon my brother, who was an accountant too, to fix the damage. It was humbling to have to sign over proxy to my brother and have him tell the IRS that the money I took from my business, $50,000 was spent on lobster and other delicacies that ultimately were flushed down a porcelain toilet bowl. I vomited more money in one year than most people made.... if you think that didn't get my attention... I had a serious problem.

My journey wasn't a straight path by any means...no successful person will tell you that it was a straight line...trials and tribulations of every kind are what give us the strength to rise above and find success, but at this time in my life, I was trapped, looking for answers in all the wrong places and getting no resolution to what was ailing me. Everyone was working on the symptoms and no one was addressing the problem...I finally had to admit the truth... The problem was me.

My last hospitalization in the early 90's left me on disability and disrupted every part of my life. I was physically, mentally and spiritually spent by this time and had nowhere to turn. My chiropractor was working on me one day and told me she had the answer. I had to go see Tony Robbins. I had no idea who he was, but weeks later I found myself at one of his seminars. I remember heading toward the firewalk and being by his side when I asked him, "can this stuff help me stop my bulimia?" I do not remember his exact answer, but I can still see the smile that came across his face with reassurance that I was in the right place. That weekend was the start of a new beginning. He took us through the life changing Dickens regression process which laid bare all that I had been hiding, opening me up to stop the sabotage I was inflicting on myself and others. Please hear what I am about to say: Up until that point, I knew with no doubt whatsoever, that I was in this world alone...that no one else suffered the way I did, that no one else was as broken as me, that everyone else had their life figured out and that I would never find my answers. This was my problem. I could never understand why my family would get caught up in my business and make such a big deal of it. I wasn't harming them, it was all about me...and I was good at it...wasn't I? I was successful, wasn't I? I was as happy as anyone else, wasn't I? If I didn't tell them, my problems were my secret... Or were they?

The trouble with the raw, unvarnished truth...is that once you really look at it, it won't go away. I had to move... I decided to enroll in Tony's mastery program and spend the year under his tutelage, getting to know my true self and learning to love my strengths and dance with my fears. By the time I got to Hawaii for the next training, I had achieved a few months of abstinence from hurting myself with the binging and purging. My "willpower" had gotten me that far, but when I engaged in combat with my internal demons, old patterns of binging and purging returned with vicious strength. I shared my horrible night with my friend the next morning, who thankfully, saw through my tough act and realized my precarious emotional state. To my surprise she decided to out me to the trainers at the seminar. That afternoon Tony was looking for someone in the audience that was suicidal...what is interesting about being that close to the edge is the quiet... the quiet terror of hopelessness... those people do not stand up and admit that they are at risk. Those people have already decided... I sat there and watched him asking different participants in the audience questions, as if to interview them to see if they were serious. My friend knew... she saw it... she felt my energy and was compelled to help me. She begged me to raise my hand... I just sat there... She persisted, nearly hysterical in her realization of my surrender. From my numb state, I began to sense the attention of 2,500 people in the audience converging on me as Tony studied me. I did not ask for this...I did not want this... I just wanted to be left alone to numb some of my sadness... How could this be, did I raise my hand, was my friend motioning to him, what happened? I cannot explain it still, I can only be thankful that the universe brought Tony and his healing energy into my circle that day. Tony is a giant of a man... both in stature and in heart... He starts asking me questions and I answered them with apprehension. Before I knew it I found myself on stage with Tony Robbins, I won...or lost depending on how you see it! I was the most obviously f'd up person among 2,500 people. LOL. I cannot describe how thankful I am that today I can laugh out loud about it... but at the time it was not even a little funny. I count those next 5 hours as one of the greatest blessings in my life. With Tony's help, I was able to shed my armor and deal directly with my pain so that I could stop hurting myself. We worked through...remember in 5 hours, what 13 years of therapy had never touched. After twenty long years of conditioning and abuse, change was a fight.

Tony taught me to break and banish the emotional ties and beliefs I held on to that were no longer serving me, giving me the freedom to find my healthier path to a fulfilling life. That was almost 20 years ago now. Tony helped give me back my life. Today, I continue in my own healing journey and have dedicated my life to empowering others with the same gift.

At the time I was slowly killing myself, I was convinced that I had it all figured out. I am still astonished by what I managed to do on the outside while inside I was dying. Despite my insanity and self-perpetuating madness, I managed to become extraordinarily successful, but I paid an enormous price….a price that far exceeded what I made financially in any lifetime... and to put that into perspective, I have made many millions.

After my experience on Tony's stage, I became aware of my patterns, realized it was easier to focus on the weight than what was really bothering me. So many do that without ever realizing it. Here is the truth... please hear it, say it with me, memorize it, embrace it... It's never about your weight, it's never about the food, and it's never about your size. The problem is always rooted in what's eating at you inside, what you are fighting to hold in, cover up, and avoid feeling. I tried to be what other people wanted me to be to fit in, to do the right thing and I was taken advantage of while trying to be accepted. I spent my whole life thinking I had to look a certain way and act a certain way. I felt unloved, unattractive and possessed a lot of self-hatred. The only thing that was really fat on me was my brain. It was full of stuff that was put there by well-meaning family, friends, media, newspapers, TV, society, all telling me how I should look to be loved and accepted by others.

Many mistakenly believe eating disorders magically end at age 25. The truth is...they exist at every age, in fact, 50 Is the New Body Hate Prime with 13% of older women suffering severe eating disorders. Many studies have proven the destructive impact of media on women's growing dissatisfaction with our bodies as we age. The average person sees over 5,000 ads a day, most of which dictate how we are supposed to look. When 26% of all commercials feature women unrepresentative of reality, the damage is devastating to every generation of women, young and old. When I was young, the average age that girls began worrying about weight was 14... today, our 8 year old babies are already worrying about their weight... and those babies grow into women who continue to believe that they are damaged and unlovable... such destructive brainwashing.

They have surveyed thousands of women and no matter how beautiful they were, they were never happy with their physical appearance. Why do I tell you this? Because so many of us live in our own palace of pain, convinced that we are alone in our struggle, but the fact is... we're not alone. Nearly every woman judges themselves by the scale, by how they look or by whatever else they believe is wrong with them...and it just has to stop. We are never skinny enough. We are never good enough, we find fault and it has become epidemic.

Then you look in the mirror, what do you see? In my pain, I decided I was fine... but let me give you my version of fine and see if it might match your own definition...I was having such a hard time with everything; I was overwhelmed and I didn't know how to communicate anymore... I thought no one was listening. People would ask, "How are you doing Lisa" and I would always reply, "I'm fine". Eventually someone caught on to my lie about being fine all the time... They asked "what do you mean fine? What's fine?" And I said again, "I'm fine". Thankfully, they pushed back, "what's fine?" I finally admitted, "I'm F*@%*d Up, Insecure, Neurotic & Emotional... I'm FINE." How long has your fine meant the same? There are so many of us out there that are feeling this way and hurting themselves, the obvious are those women that are overweight, or too skinny. The scary part is some figured out ways to hurt themselves so that we can't physically see their scars. They are the ones I am most concerned about because thousands die every day from these challenges. It hurts to see so many women suffering and from self-hatred when we are the most beautiful creatures put on this earth and made perfect just the way you are. We need to learn to be grateful for the gifts that have been given to us and focus on what we have, not what we have not.

I used to stuff my feelings with food and missed so many years of my life obsessed with something I thought meant love when it only meant destruction. I learned that secrets kill the one holding them and I was holding on for dear life. In hindsight, almost 20 years later, after looking back to that part of my life, I can tell you why I stayed sick for so many years and why so many women are still struggling today. First, I had too much invested in being sick because it became part of my identity. Have you ever done that? "I can't go out", "I don't feel good" or "it's just not a good day" or "I feel fat", "I have a headache" or "I'm so stressed I just want to be left alone", "if I were only thinner my life would be perfect". Having challenges I found others would be nice to me, so unconsciously at the time, I created tons of them. Second, if I had disabilities then it was not my fault. I had asthma so I couldn't run around and do sports, or my back hurts and I don't want to do anything, I'm in too much pain. Eventually, things that started out as my friend, like food, in order to gain control in my life became my arch-enemy. Finally, I made a decision to stop blaming my circumstances and situations, and get out of the vicious cycle. I started taking responsibility. I turned my life around and so can you! Today when I'm asked, "How are you?", I reply...I'm FAB... and my greatest wish for you and every woman in this world who has ever doubted their own worth... will find the blessing of moving from fine to FAB.

You know my whole life was based on a scale and a tape measure to see how big I was and fitting into this image I was supposed to be. I really was fine. It really became something of a joke when people would say "how are you?" and in later years, "I would say fine" and they would ask "which one yours or mine?"

So I'm going to share with you how to go from fine to fab... and the truth is... this is quite fun, because you are already FAB, Fabulous, Awesome and Beautiful, you just may need help seeing the truth of your FABULOUSNESS. This book is my expression of gratitude and my attempt to pay forward all of the healing that I have received. It is my invitation to join me on this journey of loving and accepting yourself right now, today, so that you can decide your own truth, not what the advertisements tell you. Please accept my gift to you of a proven system to help you embrace your extraordinary life with your own rules, beliefs, values and strategies for who you want to be, how you want to look, what you want to do. You are more than enough. You are FAB, Fabulous, Awesome and Beautiful.

Chapter 1

I Didn't Come With Baggage,
I Came With a Trunk

We all have our baggage. But me? I didn't come with baggage; I came with a trunk that weighed me down so much I couldn't get up. I stuffed it with everything that  ever happened to me from birth – every wrong that had been done, all of my fears, my shame, and yes, all the blame. Yes, I was doing F.I.N.E.! I was "f*@%*d up, insecure, neurotic, and emotional!" but I wasn't fine.

Now, I know I'm not alone in this. Funny, isn't it, how we believe we need to hold on to everything in our lives? We hold on to the good and the bad, the ugly along with the beautiful.

There were days when I unpacked my big trunk and would start looking over and reliving my past. It was like watching a really bad movie, you know where the ending is too painful, but you keep watching it anyway? That's what thinking about my past was like. Yet, I "watched" the movie over and over.

When you see a movie that's awful, what do you do? Do you flip the channel or leave the theater? You certainly don't buy the DVD or go back to the theater to watch it again, do you? But that's what we do with the movies of our past. We replay them over and over in our heads,

13

reminding ourselves of our failures, shame, disappointments, and what others (or our own judgments) have defined as our shortcomings. All of this negativity becomes reality because we rewind it so many times that we see it as fact, no matter whether it's based on truth or not.

"What you focus on Expands." – Unknown

As a result, I focused only on what was wrong and not what was right. A word, situation, or conversation could send me back to a place of insecurity that I thought I had put away long ago. I retreated and felt powerless despite all I had accomplished.

Maybe you have noticed how the poor seem to keep getting poorer, and the rich keep getting richer. This is because people with negative attitudes tend to keep getting dealt the worst hands in life. And complainers never run out of things to complain about no matter what good things happen to them.

There are those that suffer silently. They hold in all their feelings of failure, shame and resentment. Some eat over it, drink, spend or get depressed, but never speak a word, wanting the world to think they are perfect. Being depressed is spending too much time thinking about the way things are now and not enough time thinking about how they want things to be. Inside they are hurting and would never let anyone know.

Are you one of those people? Do you feel unworthy? Do you beat yourself up for years for what you *could* have, *should* have, or *would* have done? Do you find it hard to see the good in life? Do you find yourself complaining a lot? Do you find yourself depressed?

If you are still focusing on and blaming someone or something else for your troubles, you are carrying unnecessary baggage – maybe even an oversized trunk like I did! While you are wallowing in your sorrows, the people you blame are going about their lives happy and free. You, on the other hand, have become a prisoner in your own story and have locked yourself in that trunk.

"Hate only hurts the person carrying it" –Howard Dail

Maybe you have even found other ways to add weight to your baggage. Many people pick up disempowering habits. I certainly did. Do you turn to food, overeating, binging, purging, smoking, drinking, or spending money when you are not happy or feel the need to escape?

I can remember food and dieting playing an important role in my life since I was a teenager, but looking back now I know it started much earlier than that. My family always had challenges with food. Dad and mom tried every diet from Weight Watchers, Cambridge, Shaklee, Grapefruit diet, Nutrisystem and I was there for their journey. I remember going with dad to the meetings to learn how to cook for him as an early teenager. The refrigerator would then be stocked with low calorie and fat free foods and treats...for a little while. Mom used to tell me, don't ever look like me so I equated that to "don't ever get fat because I won't be loved". Being fat was bad. So I used to tell her if I ever look like you they should shoot me. It became one of my biggest fears based on the pain I saw her in. At my sweet 16 party, I

15

celebrated being a size 4-5. Unfortunately the fixation of having to be thin didn't die there. By the time I was old enough to drive, I went to my first Weight Watchers meeting. When I stood up, at 5"2 110lbs looking for help to lose weight, I left with my head down low after being laughed at by the crowd. I tried every diet and always looked for the next diet that would magically make me worthy of love and respect. My mantra in life was, "When I lose 10 pounds, then I'll be happy... Then I'll be skinny... Or then I'll be okay. ..Then I'll be enough, everyone will be nice to me." As quick as a blink of the eye, the years blew by and I found myself eating everything I could find. I was always on a diet, starving myself, and then all of a sudden I would have this irresistible craving and would go for some of my favorite foods like Entenmann's banana cake or mint chocolate chip ice cream. But, I wouldn't just have a bowl of ice cream. I would have the whole container and the whole cake in one sitting. I was what people would call a binge eater. There were periods where I was eating all the right foods but when I went off, all hell broke loose. What a swing, before I knew it I had gained 20 pounds. I yo-yo dieted, giving up so many times only to stuff my face with everything in sight.

The truth is: It's never about your weight, the food, or the money. The challenge is, it is easier for us to focus on the symptom than the real problems that are bothering us. The real problem of what's eating at you inside. It's about the baggage you're holding onto and hiding behind. It's about what you're trying not to feel.

Most people are looking for ways to stuff their feelings. Clearly, I'm no stranger to it. So, what did I do to turn my life around? After years of disordered and compulsive eating, binging, purging, and going through horrific hospitalizations and terrifying experiences, I finally decided to change the channel. I recognized that my childhood movies were stories I told myself that had nothing to do with who I am or the person I had become. I made a conscious decision to change from fine to FAB: Fabulous, Awesome, and Beautiful.

You can do the same. It's time to make some changes, and it starts with a decision to throw out the baggage, empty the trunk, and travel light. You cannot change what happened to you in the past, but you can change the meaning you give it. Those excuses from the past have held you back long enough. It's now time to eliminate what no longer serves you. As you read the pages that follow, I will guide you in creating some new, more empowering stories so that you can start living a more fulfilling life now.

The truth about your trunk is that there is an opening at the top, and it's wide open. To help you step out of the trunk and into a fabulous future, I'm going to share some action steps throughout the book that will help you change your life quickly, now.

"Everyone you meet comes with baggage.
Find someone who loves you enough to help
you unpack." – Author unknown

ACTION STEPS

If you want to begin your transformation, start with these questions. Figuring out the answers can change your life now!

✓ *Are your stories serving you or holding you back?*

✓ *Are you willing to do whatever it takes to change your stories now?*

✓ *Begin to pay attention to the negative stories you tell yourself. Write them down whenever you remember to do so, and begin to take stock of the baggage in your trunk.*

✓ *What has these stories or baggage cost you, your family, friends and career?*

Chapter 2

Freeing Yourself from What Holds You Back

When people used to ask me, "How are you doing?" I had an automatic answer. "I'm fine," I'd say. After all, I was trying to fit into this image of what I thought I was supposed to be. Eventually, someone said, "What do you mean 'fine'? What's 'fine' mean?" So, it became a joke for me to say, "I'm fine – F*@%*d Up, Insecure, Neurotic, and Emotional." That answer was a lot truer at that time than the lower case simple answer of "fine."

That's how the *fine* acronym was born.

Then, I began to do the work to transform my life. Trying to please the world and pleasing no one in the process – especially myself – was no longer acceptable. Learning to love myself first and end self-sabotage was a challenge, but it was well worth the fight. Believing in myself, without needing the approval of others, offered me a freedom I could have only imagined in fairy tales before.

I stopped binge eating, and I reached my ideal weight and size. Today, I'm the happiest I've ever been. It has been almost 20 years of abstinence from binging and hurting myself. Now, I eat to live; I don't live to eat. I went from fine to FAB – Fabulous, Awesome, and Beautiful – and you can, too.

Later, after my friends had become accustomed to my answer of "fine," they sometimes asked, "Which one –

yours or mine?" After I became FAB, I could safely say, "Yours." I really was by then "fine" and no longer only "*fine.*" I want the same for you.

Through the concepts in this book, you will begin to learn the 7 Secrets to moving away from depression, disordered eating and self-sabotage and how to love and accept yourself just the way you are right now. Then you can decide what's right for you, not what others tell you are right, or what advertisements and the media deem normal.

We're here now to discuss what is working today and what is not and why it isn't working anymore. Ultimately the outcome is for you to walk away with the new behaviors, strategies and beliefs to help you stop hurting yourself and overcome self-sabotage that you can apply immediately, easily and naturally to live a happier life now. It is a guide to help you make quick changes and avoid a long slow process sought by many through therapy. By helping you learn to change more quickly you can have more time to feel good instead of bad and do what's really important in life.

For years psychologists have tried to figure out *WHY* people do what they do and act in destructive ways. The difficulty in this is it never stopped them doing it. I personally went that route and it only got me angrier while I relived all my problems. It doesn't work. So knowing why we do something is not enough. If knowing was enough, we would all be skinny and rich. I am sure you know the difference between healthy and unhealthy food but that cake, muffin, candy bar will still find its way into your mouth. You know how to clean your home but you may not do it. Today there is a "how to" on everything. All you need to do is Google it or search YouTube and you can learn anything you want to know. They have been trying for hundreds of years since Sigmund Freud came up with the idea that if you could understand your problems somehow or other, they would just disappear. At the time it was brilliant and it's been revised since in numerous forms. The belief was that if we understood the psyche we could produce change. The problem is most people know why they do things but still do not change. Knowing isn't enough, it doesn't deal with the real problem.

People who overeat might have started because it would make them *"feel better"*. They know that it is unhealthy, yet they continue to overeat. The real problem is that they developed a bad habit and it manifested from doing it over and over again. Over eating isn't the problem, it is the symptom. Just as alcohol isn't the problem. They are just the drug of choice that will make them feel a certain way. When they change their connection to it, the problem goes with it.

It amazed me to learn how people acquire problems so quickly, but think it takes years to get rid of them. I remember developing a fear of eating ice cream with nuts on it because once when I was younger I choked on a walnut. I didn't eat anything with nuts for years. Today I don't have that fear. I know people who were afraid to drive over bridges or on highways due to something that happened once and they learned to create a fear around it that lasted a lifetime. It only takes one close call in a plane for someone to develop an airplane phobia. If someone can develop a fear in such a short time, it only makes sense that we can change it as quickly as it came. The belief that you have to suffer and it should take a long time to change is just a story most people were told or choose to believe. The truth is you can change your story and your belief in an instant if you want to.

It is pretty obvious to me now why I was the way I was over the years, some bad things happened to me and I kept reliving it and thinking about it every day as something would trigger that memory and reinforce my belief. I played the victim and thought to be a survivor. My depression, emotional or disordered eating, self-sabotage wasn't based on what happened. It was based on what I did with what happened. I generated it from the bad questions I asked myself every morning when I got up until I went to bed. I did a lot of "stinkin thinkin". I would ask myself the following questions, *"What's wrong with me?"* and "why me?" I would come up with the same answers all the time, *"I am never enough"*. I would see examples all around that supported that notion.

I spent years trying to figure out *WHY* to no avail, I just had to *STOP*. I had to start taking responsibility for my life good or bad. I had to *decide*. I put an end to any other option and made up my mind to move forward or die. Not moving forward was death to me; *I got sick and tired of being sick and tired.* Until I *forgave myself and others that wronged me,* I couldn't move on. The thought of doing this in the beginning seemed harder than holding onto the anger I had been accustomed to all those years, but to my surprise it was easier. I had no idea the pain, frustration and resentment that I had created was far worse than what was bestowed on me. Much of it was unfounded. When I released the anger from the past, of which I could not change, I opened myself to a world of opportunity.

I was here because of my thinking. My thinking dictates my decisions. Decisions are choices and every choice I made led me to where I am today. You may think where you are is not your fault, but I would beg to differ. Everything that happened in my life was a result of a choice I made. Years ago I chose what friends to have, where I was going to college, the courses I would take, what I would major in, where I would take my first job. I chose who I was going to date and who I was going to marry. I didn't always choose wisely, but I learned as quickly as I decided to do something that didn't serve me, I could decide and choose to do something that did. I had the power of choice. More important I had to develop a new muscle and make it a habit to choose being happy, grateful and enough.

If you have been ashamed, afraid or angry all your life, you may think it difficult at first to just *be happy*. In that case you can build it, that's what I did. I found role models of others that had what I wanted and have done it before me. I created images of what I thought happy would look like. I started to think differently. I surrounded myself by those that could guide me and were going in the direction I wanted to be. I then started to ask myself better questions. My better question for the last 20 years has been *"How can I give back to the world the gifts god has already given to me?"* *A lot more empowering wouldn't you agree?*

When you start asking good questions, you make new pictures in your head. When they are good pictures, you will feel good. If you are looking for problems, you will find them. On the other hand when you ask quality questions, *"What's good about this?"* you'll find it. When we think in a way that will get us the results we want we are happier.

This is not a new notion. Thinking and visualizing has been practiced for centuries by great athletes,

23

champions and professionals. They modeled success and saw themselves there before they ever achieved their greatness. They thought in a way that moved them forward and passed their fears. It is not enough to tell someone to just stop being afraid; you have to teach him what makes fear dissipate and then have a vision to move toward.

What I'm going to share with you is literally worth millions, because it was for me. I'm no stranger to self-sabotage. As a matter of fact, I've spent the better part of my life being an expert at it. Looking at me now you might not believe that's true but it is. When I found the secret on how to stop hurting myself, my career, my life, my relationships, my finances, everything improved considerably. So I'm going to share with you what seems easy for me but hard for others. A lot of people are going in circles. I was fortunate someone gave me help and guided me in the right direction when I needed it. Now based on where I am in my life, I feel compelled to repay that generosity and help others overcome some of their challenges and stop doing depression, disordered eating and various forms of self-sabotage. Ultimately the outcome is for you to walk away with the tools that you can apply immediately, easily and naturally to live a happier life now. I suggest you use this as a work book doing the exercises illustrated to take action immediately.

Find a blank page and draw a line down the middle, then draw two columns on the left side where you'll write down actions you'll be taking in your personal and/or professional life and on the right the dollar value it will equate to in your life. This will help you quickly free yourself from all that holds you back. For some of you it will be thousands and for others it will be millions of dollars added to your bottom line, quality of life and generations to come.

Are you sick and tired of being sick and tired?
Are you fed up with the old stories?
You can change your life forever starting now!

You have to take back control of your life in order to have the future you desire. As we come to understand the patterns that underlie self-sabotage you will begin to feel free and allow yourself to live with greater success and fulfillment.

Who This Is For

Smart people. There are many people who are smart and successful in some areas but not with themselves. Perhaps you want to stop the vicious cycle that has been passed down through generations before you and rewrite the book. If you are looking to break through the barriers that weigh you down and create more empowering alternatives in all aspects of your life, then this is for you.

It's also for **O**ver **T**hinkers. The one who thinks about everything, what's good and bad. They think themselves into stagnation, frustration, exhaustion, anxiety and even illness. As a rule, thinking is a good thing and while some people don't do it enough, others over-think everything. Not only do they have a history of *almost* doing things but more often than not they are obsessive, compulsive with perfectionist tendencies. They worry too much about nearly everything.

This is also for those who want more out of life; they feel they are **N**ever **E**nough. Not smart enough, skinny enough, pretty enough or rich enough, you know who you are. Maybe there is something holding you back and you just don't know what it is yet, you will find some of your answers here.

This is especially for our **P**eople **P**leasers that have a hard time saying "NO" to others and looking for approval and acceptance. Many times we stay where we are because we are looking at others for approval and don't want to tip the apple cart. Understand how when you say "Yes" to others, you may be saying "No" to yourself. Uncover how it is serving you and learn how to easily change it.

Studies found that people who seek or desire acceptance and/or approval from people, and/or that you have a hard time saying "NO" usually have a poor self-image.

Finally, it's for those that **G.I.T.O.W.**, who finds ways to "Get In Their Own Way" of success. You don't need other people to sabotage your dreams or goals; you can do that all by yourself. Even when things are great you look for ways to sabotage it. You are highly skilled in the art of self-sabotage and if anyone will get in your way, it's yourself.

Millions of People are Depressed

The truth is, if you are binge eating, not at your ideal weight, or unhappy, you are probably somewhat depressed. It's an epidemic in our society.

We live in a rich country where we have vast opportunities, but so many people are still not happy. Antidepressant medications are dispensed almost like aspirin. In fact, in the last 15 years, the number of people seeking treatment for depression in the United States has doubled to more than 25 million per year.

According to recent research, 90% of these people leave their doctor's offices with a prescription for antidepressants but remain depressed. Meanwhile, a study in England has shown that only people with severe depression respond to antidepressants. That's right – people who are mildly depressed or suffer from a  moderate level of depression do not get better when they take antidepressant medications!

England's managed care system now restricts doctors from prescribing antidepressants to anyone except those with severe depression. Despite this study, however, the medications continue to be prescribed to people in the U.S. with mild or moderate depression – even though the meds don't work.

Think about how many people you know on anti-depressants who are still depressed. You may even be one of them. I certainly was. It was almost 30 years ago when I was first prescribed an antidepressant. The adverse reactions I experienced were unreal. One pill made me want to pull my skin off. Another made me feel like a zombie. Even a low dose pill which managed to improve my anxiety still left me with my depression.

Prozac, the bestselling antidepressant taken by over 40 million people back in 2008, doesn't work, along with similar drugs in the same class. As reported by the

Guardian in the United Kingdom, patients improved just as much when they took a placebo (a sugar pill).

One of the steps I took 20 years ago to go from fine to FAB was to stop letting the doctors practice medicine on me. I loved my doctor, but most doctors have been taught that a prescription is the answer to every challenge.

My decision wasn't easy, though. At the time, I was on disability from work and my COBRA insurance plan (subsidized insurance at my prior company's rates) had lapsed. My prescriptions for depression, anxiety, asthma, high blood pressure, and ulcers were suddenly more expensive than my rent and more in line with what some people pay for their mortgage.

Of course, my pharmacist panicked when I made that decision, and I'm not suggesting that you follow my lead and stop taking meds without consulting a physician. But that's what I did.

I also evaluated my diet, changing what I ate to a low glycemic lifestyle and adding isotonic capable supplements to my regimen. When my hypoglycemia (low blood sugar, usually as a result of eating too much sugar) began to reverse, I noticed that my moods and energy level became more stable. Then, I was able to maintain my ideal weight with ease.

It was clear, though, that my depression wasn't all about what I was putting in my body. It was also about what I was allowing into my *head*. I had spent my first 30 years not standing guard at the gate letting everything into my consciousness without question, so I decided to be more discreet. I began to question everything that was offered to me whether it was a thought, opinion, theory, or fact. It was my choice whether I would accept it or not. Essentially, I came to the conclusion that I wasn't depressed; I was *"doing"* **depression**. If that was the case, I could also make the decision to *stop* **doing it**.

You know what I mean; I know you do! Think about how you feel when you are depressed. How is your body postured? Where do you place your eyes? How do you hold your shoulders? Is your breathing shallow or deep?

If you know the answers, you know how to *"do"* d*epressed*. This means that as easily as you go into the state of depression, you can also come out of it.

You can *decide* to *"do happy"* instead. Happiness is a decision for everyone anyway. It isn't a byproduct of something outside of you. So, how do you hold your body when you're happy? Is your posture different? How do you hold your head? Your shoulders? What do you think about when you're happy? Do you smile or frown? See – you also know how to *do* happy.

Two words that are the most powerful in the mind are *"I am"*, for anything you attach to them shapes your reality and you become. So, if you keep saying, "I am depressed," guess what you will be?

Whatever you attach "I am" to is what you become. Your subconscious

Nothing is *impossible...* the word itself says "I'm possible"!

— Audrey Hepburn

mind doesn't want you to be wrong, so if you say, "I'm a loser," you will be sure to lose. If you say, "I'm not enough," you'll never be enough. If you say, "No one will ever love me," you will never feel loved. It becomes your identity, who you are.

What would you rather be instead?

ACTION STEPS

✓ *Acknowledge that fear and doubt are holding you back from getting what you really want.*

✓ *Make two lists:*

   (1) What is working in my life right now?

   (2) What is not working in my life right now?

✓ *Write down emotions that you are **doing** that make you feel bad and you want to change.*

✓ *List new positive emotions you would like to **do** more often.*

"The happiness of your life depends upon the quality of your thoughts: therefore, guard accordingly, and take care that you entertain no notions unsuitable to virtue and reasonable nature." - Marcus Aurelius

---

Chapter 3

Secret #1: Acknowledging the Fear and Doubt

Sometimes it takes something huge to uproot us. Hurricane Sandy created 90 mile an hour winds mixed with rain, driving millions of people to seek shelter. Cars were banned from roads, bridges were closed, states called for emergency evacuations by the water and known flooding areas, schools announced closings and airports cancelled flights, all to the coming storm.

We were warned, many times by the news, radio, papers, internet, friends and family and still not everyone conformed to the warnings. We were told we would feel the brunt of the storm by midnight and it was only 7:30pm when we lost our electricity. Dinner by candlelight and learning how much we rely on technology, we made our way around the house and finally to bed. At around 9 p.m., a loud noise pierced through our bedroom, but there was no way we could see. It was pitch dark and the winds were whirling; it was safer to wait until the dawn to see the damage.

As we opened the blinds, we saw 100's of years uprooted by the hurricane. How could this old tree weather storm after storm for so many years and this one made her lose her footing? The roots stand over three times higher than me and with her demise she took down three other centuries of trees.

It reminded me of people, how we weather the storms and grow roots in our beliefs and don't let anything sway us too far until one day something really big comes along and you can no longer hold on to what you thought once was. While holding on for dear life we take casualties, not intending to but it can be our spouses, children, parents or loved ones. The loss of that tree is like the loss of our loved ones. We come to expect it will be there to offer protection from the elements, but it could no longer take the burden put upon it and it breaks just like our spirit.

That tree reminded me of myself. I held on to what I believed for so many years until one day I just broke down and could not bear the pain any longer. On the outside I looked strong and sturdy and was there for everyone but on the inside I was rotting away. I could no longer be there for anyone let alone myself. We hold on to things for so long and may look strong on the outside while the inside is withering away and it only takes one big occurrence in our lives to take us out of the game. Perhaps now would be a good time to look at what is holding you up?

Fear and doubt can relate to all sorts of issues – fear of failure, success, not being good enough, smart enough, pretty enough, thin enough, happy enough, loved enough, and on and on. We all have fears, but which of your fears are so strong that they hold you back?

Your fears are stories you tell yourself repeatedly that you have come to believe as truth and usually linked to something in the past that you are trying to avoid. They are most likely exaggerated, so you have to evaluate them to determine what's actually true and what is simply a belief. Think about it, how many of the worst case scenario stories have you told yourself that have actually come true? Probably not many, if any.

Many times people stay in jobs they are dissatisfied with or relationships that are not fulfilling in fear of not finding another. I can remember being in an abusive relationship for years because the person told me I would never find another that would love me as much as he did. Today I realize that I would never want anyone like that, but at the time I became paralyzed with the thought of being alone and stayed a prisoner in my own story.

How many stories are you telling yourself now? We need to see if we are over or under valuing the rewards we get from our behaviors.

Besides fears, many people have trouble letting go of past transgressions. Are you still lamenting over something that happened 20 years ago? Are you telling the same story to everybody about how something horrible happened to you? How you lived a terrible childhood and that's why you are the way you are. Perhaps your boss is a jerk and that's why you haven't succeeded. Do you hear the voice of a judgmental person in your head over and over – maybe even from childhood?

If others rent space in your head for FREE,
it's only because you have allowed it.

Do you still hear your parent or sibling calling you names, telling you what's wrong with you? Did they tell you that you would never amount to anything? That person may not be speaking to you here and now, but you are the one who chooses to keep replaying his/her voice in your head. So, the next time you blame someone for doing something to you, be sure to look at the other side of the hand that is pointing the finger. It may be you.

None of us can go back and start a new beginning, but all of us can start a new day and make a new ending. In order to gain our new day, we need to stop bringing the past into the present.

"No one can make you feel inferior without your consent." - Eleanor Roosevelt

---

A Figment of Your Imagination

It's important to understand how we process information from the outside and where our distinctions come from.

According to Alfred Korzybski, the belief is that "The map is not the territory." Korzybski thought that people do not have access to direct knowledge of reality. Instead, they have access to perceptions and to a set of beliefs that human society has confused with direct knowledge of reality. We believe what we cannot prove, and the only proof is our attachment to the story. So, the internal representations that we make about an outside event are not necessarily the event itself. In other words, **what you believe to be true may not be true at all.**

What if the stories you have been telling yourself are not true? What if things didn't happen the way you thought they did. It reminds me of listening to several people being at the same event and each describing it differently. One described it as being extraordinary, the best thing they have ever experienced, another said it lacked luster and no one enjoyed themselves, another exclaimed it was a okay. Who was right? What is true?

Your mind processes an *external* experience through the *internal*, comparing it with past experiences and making an assessment based on those experiences. So, everything is filtered through your past, and your assessments are limited as a result. You make an Internal Representation (I/R) or image of an event, which includes pictures, sounds, dialogue, and your feelings (whether you feel motivated, challenged, pleased, or excited). You then generalize and draw conclusions about the meaning of the event, filtering your conclusions through your own belief systems, values, decisions, and memories. This explains why two people can experience the same event and assess it in entirely different ways.

That Internal Representation of the event combines with your physiology and creates a state. "State" refers to your internal emotional state — happy, sad, frustrated, motivated, and so on. And the state in which you find yourself will determine your behavior.

Let's say we all went to the circus and I was in a great mood and every clown I saw made me giddy and every ride left me elated it brought me back to the fun times I remembered as a kid. Perhaps you were in an angry state because of something that happened earlier that day and you were carrying it with you. Then a clown came up to you to perform a trick and you got even angrier, it reminded you of a bad experience you had 30 years ago. You sit there motionless, you were stone cold. Your experience at the circus would therefore be very different than mine.

We literally make up inside our heads every experience we have. We don't experience reality directly, since we are always deleting, distorting, and generalizing. Essentially, we sense our *experience* of the territory and not the territory itself. We come to know that basically we don't know. We only know that images or beliefs are created.

If you find yourself doing depressed, angry, or sad, you may have created a story about some perceived horrible thing that happened to you a long time ago or about your terrible childhood. Sometimes, you play the same story in your head about how you'll never amount to anything. That story is the experience you have made it to be and not the experience from an objective reality standpoint. The good news is that since you were able to create the story in your mind, you can "destroy" it, too.

You have probably linked feeling bad to something you *do,* so it's time to change the channel and step into the present. In order to change, you need to acknowledge the fear or doubt and then question it. Is it true? Is it *really* true? Who do you have to be to believe this thought? Who would you be without this thought?

I remember thinking I was depressed for years. I used to say *"I am depressed"* all the time. Hence, I felt depressed.

Too often, we treat the symptom and not the problem. Our coping mechanisms become the presenting issue or surface problem. As psychotherapist Virginia Satir put it, "The *Presenting Issue* itself was seldom the real problem; rather, how people *coped* with the issue *created* the problem."

We need to learn how to process information and perceived problems and find more resourceful ways to deal with them. One way is to ask yourself, *"Is what I believe true?"* Another is to create something more important to *move toward* as opposed to what you struggle to *move away from*.

"It's not what's happening to you now or what has happened in your past that determines who you become. Rather, it's your decisions about what you focus, what things mean to you, and what you're going to do about them, that will determine your ultimate destiny." – Anthony Robbins

---

The Secret to Living a Happy Life

The best thing about the past is that it's over. Bad relationships and poor decisions can all be filed away, and you have an opportunity to rewrite the book and learn from them. The future has yet to be written, and you can make it whatever you want it to be.

I was so excited when I figured out what everyone ultimately wants to know, how to be happy? It is very simple, think right. The right of the brain and the quadrant.

The secret to living a happy life now is being in the present.

	Unhappy	Happy
	Past	**A**uthentic
Focus	Present	Focus
	Fear	**G**ood
	Past	Future

There's a quote by Ellen Muth that says it bluntly: "If you keep one foot in the past and one in the future, you're just pissing on the present."

Since I'm a very visual learner, that was enough for me to understand. If I wanted to live a happy life and do great things, I needed to learn to be present and look toward the future.

Living in the **P**ast. When we stay in the past and believe our negative, unhappy thoughts, all we do is create pain and suffering. What causes pain and depression is not the world around us, but what we believe about the world around us.

We live in a a world of unlimited possiblities. Yet, we fixate on a few things and don't let them go. As our unpleasant past stories manifest, they keep us from moving forward. You can't start the next chapter of your life if you keep rereading your last one.

So, if you don't like something, change it. If you can't change it, change the way you think about it. Until you put the focus on where you are and where you want to go, you will miss today. And you will never become who you want to be if you keep blaming everyone else for who you are now.

When neuroanatomist/brain scientist Jill Bolte Taylor shared how our brain works, she talked about being of "right mind." She said that the right hemisphere of the brain is all about this present moment. Right here, right now. It thinks in pictures and learns kinesthetically through the movement of the body. "In this moment, we are here, perfect and beautiful," she said. So, we need to be of RIGHT Mind – present here and now.

Of the left hemisphere of the brain, Taylor said that it thinks linearly and methodically. It's all about the past and the future, taking the enormous collage of pictures in the mind and picking out details about the present moment. It then categorizes and associates the moment with the past and projects those pictures into the future. "Our left brain thinks in language and calculating intelligence," she said.[1]

This phenomenon is responsible for our decisions and is probably where we create our painful associations to the past. The bottom line: When you're thinking with your left brain, you're not in the present.

Fears. Every fear you face is one you have learned throughout your life, except for two innate fears. We are born with these fears: loud noises and falling. They are built into our DNA and have been passed down from generation to generation as a survival mechanism.[2]

The sole purpose of these fears is to keep you alive and create emotions that will motivate you to avoid danger.

According to a survey: "In general, women are far more fearful than men. Twice as many were afraid of heights, insects, deep water, and flying or driving in cars; three times as many were frightened of darkness, and four times as many were frightened of elevators. They were also more fearful of dogs, getting sick and dying. It is worth noting that the only fear that men have more often than women is the "fear of financial problems."[3]

Let go of things that no longer serve you, and put your problems in the past where they belong. How do you do this? By questioning your fears, you cannot change what you refuse to confront.

When we eliminate fears and past stories, we can experience more happiness. (See diagram page 37)

Good Decisions come from asking better questions and changing your state. You will make thousands of decisions over your lifetime. Some will have no impact, and some will transform your world. The state you are in when you make those decisions and your thoughts at that moment will affect whether the decisions are good or bad.

"Worry does not empty tomorrow of its sorrow.
It empties today of its strength." - Corrie Ten Boom

So, start manifesting skills to develop good states. Learning to put yourself in a good mood is a starter. I find just getting up and doing something else, thinking about all I am grateful for puts a smile on my face, putting on some music, dancing like no one's watching, calling a friend, taking a walk, exercising, playing with the kids can change my state. When you're in a bad mood and have negative thoughts, you feel bad and make bad decisions. Sometimes, you just need to tell yourself to STOP!

SAYING "NO" TO BAD CHOICES
IS SAYING "YES" TO YOU!

Understanding what you have control over and what you don't is, therefore, very important. So is understanding what's worth getting upset over. I stopped watching the news 20 years ago because I got tired of hearing bad things and seeing people do stupid stuff. I used to get upset at the news and felt as if the media was just giving more people crazy ideas. I decided it was a waste of my time and energy. Where are you putting your energy that makes you feel bad? You get to choose if you want to continue doing that.

Holding onto anger or frustration for things you can't control or change is not a good decision, it is just *doing* stupid. STOP! I'm not saying you're stupid, but I'm saying you are *doing* stupid! We all do it, and it becomes an excuse to feel bad.

For example, feeling sorry for others without the ability to change the situation for them is not a good use of your time. If you feel bad about children starving in other countries, send your money there and feed them. If you feel bad about children who are abused by their parents, take one of these children into your home, and raise the child in a better environment.

Staying upset about something that happened to you 30 years ago is also useless. It will not change the past. It's over; move on. Mourning over the loss of a person will not bring that person back. Instead, celebrate that person's life by replaying wonderful memories and celebrating the gifts they brought into the world. If getting upset is not going to bring them back, *stop it*. Feeling bad and doing nothing about it is a waste of your energy.

Come from a place of gratitude for what is, and that state will make you open to what can be.

Asking quality questions will help you make better decisions, and your actions will match the results you get in your life.

Authentic to you: Making decisions for you instead of others is key. When you make decisions just to please others, you privately beat yourself up by doing something that is against your better judgment. Think about all of the decisions you have made in the past in order to make someone else happy. They no doubt left you feeling angry and resentful. Perhaps in the end, these people still weren't happy, so you sacrificed yourself for nothing.

Life isn't about pleasing everybody; it's about pleasing yourself. Follow your core purpose, and make yourself happy first. Inadvertently, when you make decisions to please others, you are not being genuine and true to you.

Most people don't love themselves because they have lost touch with who they are. It is not that you don't love yourself as much as it is, *you do not love the facade you created for yourself.* In order to be truly happy, you need to be your authentic self.

---

*"I am in charge of how I feel,
and today I choose happiness."*

Everyone deep down inside wants to be loved and accepted. The obstacle is when you try to be loved and accepted at the expense of your authentic self.

Learn how to accept yourself. That's right – accept yourself, flaws and all. Nobody is perfect, so stop trying to be perfect. I decided long ago to strive for imperfection, and I have always succeeded in meeting those expectations. As long as I'm moving forward, I'm happy.

F.L.Y. – First Love Yourself. Then, others will follow.

Trying to be someone else is a waste
of the person you are.

What Makes Some Triumphant?

Among the greatest stories in history, there are stories of peril and despair, and there are stories of triumph and victory. They are in every great movie. You hear a sob story of devastation, followed by something great that drives the person to move forward. Why is it that some people can come out of catastrophic challenges victorious, while others let those challenges define them? Why is it that some people throw in the towel when horrible things happen to them?

Here's an interesting story for you: A young girl was born into poverty in Mississippi to a teenage single mom and was later raised in inner city Milwaukee. She experienced unbelievable hardship as a child. She was raped at age nine and became pregnant at fourteen. Her mother felt she couldn't care for her daughter, so she sent her to live with the man the girl calls her father today, a barber in Tennessee. A child herself, having a child she suffers a catastrophic loss when her son dies in infancy. At this point, after being abused, neglected, and abandoned, many people would consider their life over. But this young woman decided she wanted something more. She worked hard to achieve her goals and never gave up. She continued to move forward despite controversy and decided to make something of herself. She eventually launched her own production company and became internationally syndicated. Today, Oprah Winfrey is often praised for overcoming adversity and has become an incredible role model and philanthropist to others.

"The greatest discovery of all time is that a person can change his future by merely changing his attitude." - Oprah

---

Another story that comes to mind is about a young girl born in Alabama back in the turn of the century. At 19 months old she contracted an illness described by doctors as "an acute congestion of the stomach and the brain," which might have been scarlet fever or meningitis. The illness did not last for a particularly long time, but it left her deaf and blind. Growing up and never learning how to speak or communicate her mother was unwilling to accept the fate at hand and was inspired by a reading while looking for answers to help her child. She sought expert advice everywhere and subsequently through her search was put in touch with Anne Sullivan a former student of Perkins Institute for the Blind who was visually impaired and only 20 years old, to become Helen Keller's instructor. Through Anne's persistence and dedication she opened Helen's world to all its possibilities. Helen became the first deaf and blind person to earn a Bachelor of Arts degree. Determined to communicate with others as conventionally as possible, Keller learned to speak, and spent much of her life giving speeches and lectures. She learned to "hear" people's speech by reading their lips with her hands—her sense of touch had become extremely supple. She became proficient at using Braille and reading sign language with her hands as well. Keller went on to become a world-famous speaker, author and advocate for numerous causes.

"At this moment, when Helen Keller was a child, she showed us the power of a determined human spirit and reminded us all that courage and strength can exist in the most unlikely places." - Patsy Riley

---

Now, I want to tell you a story about a young girl from a middle class family. She was never financially deprived; her parents always provided for her. Born with asthma, she always had difficulty breathing, which limited many of her activities. Both parents worked, so she was a latch key child. She took on the responsibilities of running the house, which included cooking, cleaning and doing laundry by the age of nine. Raised in a strict home and confronted with verbal abuse, she thought she had to be perfect. She became an overachiever, fearing that she would never meet expectations and feeling like she was never enough. She got good grades, didn't get into trouble, and never did drugs.

She was sexually abused for the first time as a young adult while on a date, followed by another incident of abuse a few years later by an employer. At 18 years old, she was on medications for ulcers caused by stress and became very ill. She lost 30 pounds in one month and was admitted to a hospital at 95 pounds, weak and unable to hold herself up, hooked up to IV's. Her potassium was dangerously low, and she had what they called at the time a "sudden heart attack." Diagnosed as clinically depressed as well, she was hospitalized in a psychiatric ward for a month, alongside mentally ill people who were seriously sick.

When released from the hospital, this young girl had more than a dozen prescriptions in her hands. This was the beginning of 13 years of depression, high blood

45

pressure, hypoglycemia, disordered eating, compulsive overeating, bulimia, multiple hospitalizations, and specialized doctors. Despite years of therapy and Overeaters Anonymous (OA), she still struggled.

Even through all of the controversies, she managed to graduate college with honors. She went on to create millions of dollars for Fortune 100 companies. She followed everyone's advice and worked hard, invested, lived on very little and saved for a rainy day. By the time she was twenty three she started her first business. At thirty she had amassed more than most people do in a lifetime and was semi-retired.

Then, what felt like overnight, she lost fifteen years of savings in the stock market when WCOM went bankrupt and dot coms crashed.

By the age of thirty-five she found herself desperate with over a half a million dollars in debt and nowhere to turn. She had to start over. Ready to rebuild and recoup the losses she went back to work and built a new business where she earned millions of dollars over the years and became a successful entrepreneur and teaches others to do the same.

Today she has no debt, was able to get off of all of the prescriptions, and is an international speaker, author, entrepreneur, and Licensed Master NLP Practitioner. That girl was me.

"Everything happens for a reason. I just need to wait to find out what it is." - Lisa Lieberman-Wang

---

So, how did I come out of it, when some people lose a job and end up with a shattered life? I wondered that, too, and eventually discovered that it had to do with my thinking and my beliefs.

Do you believe it's possible to triumph, or do you believe it's impossible? Whichever you believe, it will become a self-fulfilling prophecy.

Believing in Possibility

Somewhere deep down, all of those individuals who triumph over adversity do so because at the core, their beliefs and values drive their motivation to move on. They have a vision for something better – a desire for more. They are programmed or wired for success. Despite some cross wiring, there is a bigger drive to move forward than there is to move backward. Some might call it faith: seeing what you cannot prove, knowing there is more, and that there is a purpose for being. Those who don't are caught up in self-sabotage.

I used to say, "God doesn't give you more than you can handle. And I am fooling him, too." I always believed there had to be a bigger reason for bad things happening to good people. I choose to believe that I will one day find the answer for why things happen. Finally, when the timing is right, it will be revealed to me.

I went through difficult experiences so that I could one day do what I'm doing now – help others do the same thing.

What you believe determines who you will become. Those who achieve the most in their lifetime give themselves reasons why they *can* accomplish their goals instead of reasons why they *can't*.

Our behaviors and compulsions function in the present, not the past. In order to change those behaviors and compulsions, you have to do something different in the present. Then, you can replace the bad decisions and habits with new associations.

"I think the law of attraction has been misstated. You do not attract what you want. You attract what you are. That's how the law of attraction works." - Wayne Dyer

The Fundamental Elements of Self-Sabotage

Self-sabotage is a result of fear, doubt, shame, frustration, low self-esteem, and the need for the approval and acceptance of others (sometimes even through negative attention). We have become a society of fitting in rather than standing out.

Low self-esteem can affect every aspect of your life, emotionally and physically. Too many of us believe that our worth is based on how we look, how much money we make, how successful we are, or how skinny we are. Coming from this place, nothing is ever enough.

We find ways to reinforce our beliefs by spending time with other people who we allow to bring us down. Misery loves misery, and we rise to the same level of our peers. I learned quickly that I didn't

> *It's NOT what you are that holds you back,*
> *It's Who You Think You're Not!*
> -Denis Waitley

want to tolerate being around negative people who accept mediocrity. I wanted to be with leaders. I wanted to be with those making things happen, not talking about what happened. "It's not what you are that holds you back, it's what you think you are not." - Denis Waitley

48

When I first started my recovery from disordered eating, binging, and purging 30 years ago, my doctors suggested I go to Overeaters Anonymous in addition to therapy. At that time, I was open to anything that would help me stop. OA is a fellowship of individuals who, through shared experiences, strength, and hope, are recovering from compulsive eating.

For years, I sat in OA meetings with others no different from me. They, too, found ways to cope with what was hurting them. The program had many merits, but it also had its vices. Sitting in the rooms listening to others share their stories made me feel like I wasn't alone. Some stories brought me back to my own stories, and others gave me more ideas for handling difficult emotional states. I would get a short time of abstinence from binging and purging, only to go back to the insidious *dis-ease* for another quick fix. After years of white knuckling the dis-ease, I got to the point that I believed the only way to stay away from the food was to go to a meeting. But I wanted more out of my life. It was as if I put down the food, my substance of choice, and picked up meetings in its place.

For some, this is great. There are people in the rooms today for 5, 10, 20, 30 years just like at AA (Alcoholics Anonymous). It just wasn't for me. I loved the community, but I didn't like "needing" a meeting.

I felt I was reinforcing a negative state every time I'd share, "Hello, my name is Lisa, and I am bulimic and a survivor." There was nothing empowering about that at all. I wanted more. I wanted to LIVE!

Studies have proven that we are only as good as the people we spend time with. I wanted to be with people who didn't hold on to the identity of "*being a*

49

compulsive eater or survivor." I felt there was something missing. I was conditioned to move forward and needed more.

What is Disordered Eating?

A more common but lesser known challenge is **"Disordered Eating**.*"* Disordered eating affects 3 in 4 American women ages 25 to 45, who have unhealthy relationships with food or their bodies, according to a survey sponsored by SELF Magazine in partnership with the University of North Carolina at Chapel Hill.  Disordered eaters may engage in excessive dieting, eating when not hungry, eating in secret, skipping meals, and primarily eating fattening, over-processed, "comfort" or convenience foods. This can result in low energy, trouble concentrating, anxiety, depression, and/or being moderately overweight or underweight. Although disordered eating is considered less serious than eating disorders or obesity, it can lead to both.[4]

It all boils down to a state of being that we are trying to achieve through food.

Always Being Open

In the 90's after more than 10 years of looking for answers, and after several hospitalizations and nowhere to turn, my chiropractor told me that I needed to see Anthony Robbins. I had never heard of him, but while I was in her office, she made a call. Weeks later, I was at one of his seminars. That was the start of a new beginning.

I registered for his mastery program, and just months later in Hawaii that same year, he gave me the gift of a lifetime – he worked with me for five hours. His honesty and ability to see through to the real challenge I faced helped me walk through many obstacles that had impeded my success and happiness.

All those years of saying *"I am* bulimic" would have been truer only if I had said, *"I did bulimia." The actions were not who I was; they were just what I did.* This was a key distinction for me.

I decided if I couldn't change the people around me, I needed to change who was around me. I eliminated some negative people in my life and chose to stop going to therapy and OA. It doesn't mean that I may never go back to a meeting, but I choose not to exercise that habit. I have found the tools in this book to be more empowering and resourceful. They have helped me create a better quality of life.

The truth is that many people turn to food, alcohol, drugs, spending, or negative self-talk for comfort and support and in an attempt to control life and cope. All of these coping mechanisms numb feelings and cover up what is really going on inside. *It's the way we think that causes us the most pain.*

You can change your story and change your life.

"Holding onto anger is like drinking poison and expecting the other person to die." –Buddha

---

Take Care of Your Mother's Daughter

The wisest woman I have ever met, my grandma Susan, gave me great advice after she watched me nearly kill myself: *"Baby, take care of your mother's daughter."* Many of us are so good at taking care of everyone else that we neglect ourselves.

It is very easy to take care of others because when we do, the focus is no longer on ourselves. We feel needed and loved. When we are able to give, we feel we are enough. We give to our families, children, friends, even strangers in an effort to feel worthy.

Millions of people who do charity work aren't doing it for the reasons you think. They are often the ones who need love the most but are unable to give that love to themselves. So, they freely give it to others. Charity begins at home. Even on a plane, they tell you to put the oxygen mask on yourself before you take care of a minor.

When you learn to love yourself unconditionally, life changes. My grandma used to sing to me, "With all your faults, I love you still." The chorus goes, "It had to be you, wonderful you, It had to be you."

Charity changes when you do it with no strings attached. When you take care of yourself first, your charity can come from a pure heart, and you can give even more than you ever thought possible.

Isn't it time you took care of the most important person in the world – your mother's daughter? Don't you want the best for her?

Feed yourself with love, acceptance, kindness, and praise. Your body hears everything you say to it, so start taking care of it with tender loving care. Encourage it, nurture it to be your best friend, and it will be.

"The only person you are DESTINED to become is the person you DECIDE to be."- Ralph Waldo Emerson

---

ACTION STEPS

✓ ***Practice Positive Self-Talk.*** *Create new statements to replace the negative statements you say to yourself. Instead of "I'm a loser" or "I can't do this" or "No one will hire me" or "I'm not skinny enough" or "I'm not pretty enough," say empowering statements to yourself. For example, you might say, "This is easy" or "I've succeeded before, and I can do it again" or "I can do anything I set my mind to" or "If others can do it, why not me?" Make statements that put you in alignment with what you want instead of what you want to avoid.*

✓ ***Create a Goal or Vision to Move Toward.*** *Ask yourself: What is my purpose in life? What goal or vision do I want to move toward?*

"In order to let go of the fear and doubt that keeps you from moving forward, recognize that the past doesn't equal the future. Refuse to accept mediocrity, and begin to design the life you want." Lisa Lieberman-Wang

---

53

Ask yourself these questions:

1. What stories do you repeatedly tell yourself? Are they really true, or do you just believe they're true? Remember that beliefs are not necessarily truths.

2. What stories do you repeatedly tell other people? Do those stories serve you?

3. How old are the stories you tell yourself and/or others?

4. What role are you playing in your story of life? Are you the conqueror or the victim?

5. Do negative things consistently happen to you?

6. Are you a complainer, or are you the person who takes charge?

7. Do you have a tendency to take comments personally, even when they aren't meant personally?

8. How long do you dwell on a negative comment that someone has made about you? Do you forever hold it against the person who said it, or do you move on?

9. Do events happen to you or for you? For example, let's say you were detained and arrived late at your destination. Would you say this happened to you, or did the delay happen for you so that you could perhaps avoid an accident? It's a matter of perspective, isn't it?

10. Do you frequently ask, "Why me?" or "Why not me?" Do you often lament that other people get what you don't, comparing your life to the lives of others?

Chapter 4

Secret #2: Taking Inventory of Life Lessons & Beliefs

The next thing you do is take inventory of your life lessons, beliefs, and values. Why? Because they shape your reality. You use them to guide your actions and behavior, as well as form your attitudes toward your life and what happens to you. It is wonderful to know we can change beliefs and values that have been useless and lying unchallenged within us for years. You get to decide now. One of the biggest gifts we could ever be given is recognizing that we can change our beliefs and values.

Your beliefs are assumptions you make about the world. They may or may not have any basis in truth. It's a deep feeling within that we hold to be true in our mind without actual proof or evidence. Most of your beliefs were formed by the time you were five years old from external forces like your parents, teachers, friends, peers, and family.

Our core beliefs about love and security are formed while we are infants. Let's say you're a two-year-old crying in your crib and waiting to be picked up. This is a common experience all children have. However, it may be that this time you cry too long and believe that no one is coming to pick you up because you're not loved. If you were loved or good enough, someone would be there for you. Since your mother doesn't come for you, that *proves* there's something wrong with you. None of this is logical thinking, or in any way conscious, but it occurs in all of us over and over again.

When you love someone, it's easy to believe falsehoods based on what they do and say. Didn't you believe your parents when they told you Santa Claus exists?

When I first heard how much of an influence these beliefs have on our lives, I was scared. At five years old, you don't question what you are thinking or what you're being told. But as an adult, you can evaluate your beliefs and identify which ones to keep and which ones to discard.

When I was young, I believed that if something broke, it was automatically my fault. I was always reprimanded when something went wrong in the house – even if I had nothing to do with it. As a result, I started to believe that everything was my fault. If the vacuum broke, Lisa did it. If the washing machine broke, I was to blame. It wasn't until I was older that I questioned that belief. How is everything my fault? Machines break, and it isn't my fault.

I was also called bad names. I did not grow up with flowery names like "princess" or "sweet pea." The nickname I was given was not very nice. I remember owning the nickname for countless years until someone said to me, "If someone called you a chair, would that mean you are a chair?" That's silly, isn't it? Of course, I'm not a chair. So, why do we believe it when someone says we're stupid, for example? You can choose what you hold on to and what you don't. I finally let go of the labels others had given me that had nothing to do with who I am.

What about those people in our lives that we love and we still allow them to press our buttons? Just remember to not wear anything with buttons.

Your Values

Your values stem from your beliefs. They are the ideas that you hold important like integrity, honesty, loyalty, and education, to name a few. They govern the way you behave, communicate, and interact with others, and they determine your attitudes, opinions and your health.

The "placebo effect" shows just how powerful the mind can be in terms of beliefs. In many medical studies, one group of patients is given medication, while another group is given sugar pills without knowing it. Time and time again since 1955 when the phrase was coined, 50-60% of patients responded to the placebo as if they were taking the actual medication. In other words, they saw results because of the power of the *belief* that they were being treated and taking medication.

This doesn't mean that human beings are not intelligent. It just means that we are capable of deceiving ourselves with the power of our minds. We are able to fool ourselves.

One of the life lessons that I formed when I was a young girl was that men are not reliable and cannot be trusted. I was taught to make enough money on my own so that I could be independent and self-sufficient because I would never be able to rely on a man for help. The challenge then came when I wanted to be in a relationship but had a hard time relying on my partner. I ended up in relationships that supported my theory that men were not reliable or trustworthy. I never trusted they would be there for me, so they weren't.

To make matters worse, I entered a career in marketing technology which meant I was surrounded by men all the time. I experienced fear and anxiety for years from my lack of trust in men, believing that I had to watch my back in the workplace. Once I chose to change that belief, I met my husband, Yardley, who is definitely reliable and trustworthy.

Another belief I had was that I needed to make six figures to be considered successful. I was actually making six figures when I got very sick and went from making a lot of money to being on disability to making no money. All of a sudden, what made me successful no longer existed, and I felt insignificant as a result. Eventually, I learned that being myself made me successful, no matter how much money I made.

What are some of your beliefs, values, and life lessons? How many of them actually hold water if you hold them up to scrutiny?

Think about some of the things you have been told over the years. Were you told that you had to look a certain way, act a certain way, or achieve a certain status in order to be successful or even acceptable?

Only you can decide which beliefs, values, and life lessons serve you and which ones do not.

You are the sum of all of your life lessons.

You can let your lessons define you or guide you. If you let them guide you, they will take you to incredible places.

Defining Your Beliefs, Values, and Rules

Another key to living a happier life now is understanding the rules you create for yourself that stand in the way of your happiness.

We put conditions on our happiness that are contingent upon what others do, and this puts our happiness out of our own control. That's hardly a winning strategy because it sets us up for disappointment.

Let's say you want to feel love. You can just choose to feel love and take sole responsibility for it. But if you decide that you will feel love only when your husband stops hogging the remote or when your kids put away their toys, you may never feel love. Or maybe you tell yourself you'll feel happy when you get that promotion. Then, your happiness is contingent upon material things.

Feeling love or happiness is an inside job. So, set yourself up to win. For example, here are some of my rules and values for love: Anytime I see love, think about love, give love, smile, look into someone's eyes, give a hug, or see a child, I feel love. I make it easy for me to feel love all the time.

What are some of the rules you have set up before you can feel something positive? Are your emotions contingent on others playing their role the way you think they should or is it 100% on you?

Is Being Sick Costing You Happiness?

A lot of times, people receive lessons that they don't even know they're getting. There are people who literally get sick just to get attention. I had found over the years that when I got sick and was hospitalized over a month each time, everybody was nice to me. So, inadvertently, I learned to be sick. That wasn't what I consciously set out to do, but unconsciously, I did it so that I could feel loved and get attention. There was a secondary gain because I was rewarded for doing what made me feel bad. Therefore, I felt bad longer.

Some people create challenges just to escape boredom.

You might have learned that being sick or having problems all the time gets you attention. You continue to sabotage yourself because if you have a problem, everybody pays attention to you. The only challenge is that you always have to have a problem, or you'll never get attention. Hence, you'll never stop having problems.

People who do this don't realize they're doing it, and soon, their family and friends get tired of hearing their problems. **Decide what beliefs will guide you.**

ACTION STEPS

✓ *What beliefs will I choose to believe and guide my future?*

✓ *What actions do I take to get attention and feel love? Is it giving me the love I really want?*

✓ *I will create new rules so that I have 100% control over my happiness.*

Chapter 5

Secret #3: Breaking Through Toxic Emotions and Meanings

It is fascinating to learn that the language you associate to things creates your circumstances. Most of us aren't even aware that we are the culprit to our dilemmas.

There are almost 1,000,000 words in the English language. [5,6,7] Yet, we use only 2,000 words, including the short words like "at" and "the." With so many available words, you'd think we'd all have bigger vocabularies. There are more than 4,000 words to describe emotions, some of them are positive to empower and others are negative, disempowering emotions, but the average person generalizes and uses less than a dozen. [8] They then link these words to the same pain or pleasure.

Therefore, we create the same few states and feelings regardless of the experience. When someone says; "I can't get a break" or "Everything happens to me," see what happens when they use the same words to describe different circumstances. For example: If a bad incident happens and creates a lot of emotion and anguish, you might attach the meaning, "Everything happens to me." Every time anything happens, you say, "Everything happens to me" even if the incident is a small thing.

Maybe the first incident was indeed a horrible accident that wasn't your fault, so you felt, "Everything happens to me." The next incident, though, might just be that you order a muffin and receive the wrong one. Still, you turn around and say, "Everything happens to me." Because you're using the same expression and words, you feel the same anxiety, frustration, anger, and pain as you did when you had the accident.

The meaning you give to an incident creates the emotion you feel about it. The words used are so critical. Change the words, change the meaning, change the emotion, change the action, and change the result. What we experience is based on the words and emotions tied to it.

See things as they are not worse than they are. Stop making everything a big catastrophe and focusing on it as if it's the end of the world. The likelihood that it's the worst thing that ever happened to you is low.

Acknowledge that there are other words to describe your experiences. Stop generalizing or seeing your circumstances in absolutes "Everything," "always," or "never" or you will feel the same intensity you did the first time you used it.

When you find new words to describe a feeling, you'll find new emotions and won't sabotage yourself.

It's also not a good idea to assume what other people are thinking. We're usually wrong when we assume. I can remember countless times when I wondered what my husband was thinking. I made up elaborate stories in my head and sometimes even reacted to my own story, feeling frustrated with him. Then, when I asked him what he was actually thinking, he said "Nothing." I knew that couldn't be possible. How can anyone ever not be thinking? I believed he wasn't telling me the truth, so I probed for more. I have never not been thinking of something. My mind never stops and turns off. How does he do that? Before I knew it, I created a situation that never existed except in my head. He was really not thinking of anything. Studies have shown that men can do that. It amazed me, but it's true.

Another suggestion is to learn to reframe patterns. We create patterns that determine our meaning and the state in which we live. Reframing a pattern allows you to see it from a different perspective.

"Our greatest battles are with our own minds."
- Jameson Frank

We often blow things out of proportion. I've seen people go into road rage just because someone has cut them off, even if it wasn't intentional. Learning to reframe can be very therapeutic. Maybe this person didn't cut you off intentionally but was going to miss his exit and didn't know how else to get home. Or you could look at it this way: "Was I ever lucky that I didn't hit him; someone was watching over me!" You can reframe anything by changing your perspective and self-talk.

Then, there are words you want to avoid which become very toxic to your emotions. The following words and phrases are **disempowering and instill doubt and pain** in all of us:

I can't	Try
Could have	But
Should have	Might
Would have	If

Words like these potentially negate the positive suggestions you give yourself. If you get rid of these words, you will eliminate self-sabotage and stop berating yourself for being imperfect.

Challenge yourself for a week to write these words down any time you say one of them. If you say "I can't," write it down. Stop yourself. Wait until you see how many times you use these words in your vocabulary, and you'll understand that you can't accomplish your goals because you keep telling yourself you can't. Remember, your unconscious doesn't know the difference between what's real and what you tell yourself. So, if you say you can't, you're right!

I think what messes up most people are the perfect pictures in their minds of how things are supposed to be.

DON'T Hear DON'T

Your mind is so astonishing. It doesn't recognize the word "DON'T." Did you ever notice, if you have a teenager and say, "Don't stay out past curfew!" What do they hear? "Stay out past curfew." **The brain does not process the word "don't."**

Here's an idea: If you want to trick your teenager, say "Don't come home before your curfew." Then, they'll come home before their curfew.

The "don'ts" are pretty intriguing. Use it in your vocabulary to be persuasive, not ineffective. Embedding the DON'T command can take advantage of the situation. For example, in real estate, you can say, "Don't think about those houses and how quickly they are selling." Urgency is built this way. Think of all the other ways you can use the word effectively to get what you want.

It takes 20 positive statements about yourself to counteract just 1 negative statement you've said to yourself about you.

Every time you put yourself down and say you're not pretty enough, smart enough, rich enough, or whatever, it takes 20 positive statements to counteract that one negative comment. Stop programming yourself with the negative, and stay positive. I just love this illustration. See how we use our emotions to give incorrect meanings to objects and circumstances? Before I sought help to get a handle on my food and weight problem, I weighed myself every day (sometimes twice a day). If the number wasn't a good one, I would move the scale around the room to a different location to see if it would give me a better number. It sounds crazy, and it was. I would beat  myself up over a number. I missed out on being with friends and doing things because I was having a FAT day. Do you know anyone like this? Are *you* like this?

If your day is good or bad based on the number on the scale, I suggest you get rid of the scale! If you are presently on a journey to lose weight, have someone weigh you once a month – no more. Your clothes will let you know without the scale if you're on the right track.

When I was in the hospital, they weighed us every day with our backs to the scale so that we couldn't see the number. At the end of the week, they showed us the daily log they kept. It amazed me to see that the morning after having a Chinese dinner, I could see the difference of 3-5 lbs, but by the end of the week, it always averaged out to the same number.

There are many reasons the number on the scale might go up. The obvious one is that you're eating fattening or sugary foods or drinking alcohol. Other factors can be water retention from salty foods or that time of the month for women. It can be an inflammation reaction to something you ate. There are numerous explanations, but when you merely use a number as the deciding factor as to whether you're okay or not okay … well, that is NOT OKAY!

Life improves when you get rid of the negative meanings you have ascribed to objects and situations.

Conquering Negative Thoughts with Affirmations

Affirmations are statements or thoughts that describe a desired situation and are repeated many times in order to program your subconscious mind and trigger it into action. You have the power to transform yourself based on what you think, and affirmations are a way of gradually changing your thinking.

Every thought you think and every word you say is an affirmation – whether positive or negative. Your self-talk or inner dialogue is a stream of affirmations. You are continually subconsciously affirming beliefs with your words and thoughts. Your beliefs then create your life experience in every moment.

Your beliefs are just learned thought patterns that you have developed since childhood. Many of these beliefs work well for you, but others may be working against you, sabotaging you from achieving what you want.

Everything you think or say is a reflection of your inner truth and beliefs. Remember that many of these so-called "inner truths" may not actually be true at all. Often, they're based on inaccurate impressions that were constructed when you were a child without the ability to accurately assess situations.

"The brain we develop reflects the life we lead. This has far-reaching implications for the effects of habitual behavior in our lives." These are the words of Sharon Begley in her book; *Train Your Mind, Change Your Brain*.[4] Groundbreaking documentation supports the idea that we can *change our brains by changing our thoughts*. The results are astounding. These breakthroughs in our understanding show it is possible to "reset our happiness meter, regain the use of limbs disabled by stroke, train the mind to break cycles of depression and OCD (Obsessive-Compulsive Disorder) and reverse age-related changes in the brain."[9]

Studies show that we have anywhere from 12,000 to 60,000 thoughts per day. But according to some research, as many as 98% percent of these thoughts are exactly the same as we had the day before. Talk about creatures of habit!

67

Even more significant, **80% of our thoughts are negative.** No wonder so many people are unhappy. Each pessimistic thought or word is a negative affirmation and can be even more powerful than positive affirmations because we often find these pessimistic thoughts easier to accept.

Negative thoughts are particularly draining. Complaints, whining thoughts containing words like "never," "can't," and "should," or thoughts that diminish your sense of self-worth, produce corresponding chemicals that weaken your body. No wonder we're burned out at the end of the day!

Having a positive mindset is one of the most powerful life strategies to living a happier life. You spent your whole life developing a negative mindset. It might be a good idea to invest some time in creating a positive one.

Your subconscious mind uses the behavior patterns you have learned over the years to automatically respond and react to different everyday events in your life. This is essential for your survival; you need to be able to respond quickly to events around you which would be impossible if you had to inspect every aspect of every event.

Our learned responses and thought patterns enable us to automatically respond to circumstances quickly and easily. Problems arise when our beliefs are formed from a distorted perspective that was developed at an early stage of our lives. The strategy that built the foundation might have been appropriate for a difficult incident as a child, but inappropriate for succeeding as adults.

What are Positive Affirmations?

Positive affirmations are usually short positive statements, so they are easy to remember and targeted toward a specific set of beliefs. They are designed to challenge and undermine negative beliefs, replacing them with positive self-nurturing beliefs. Affirmations are a kind of "brainwashing" except you get to choose which negative beliefs to wash away.

It's imperative to remember to speak and think positively because your subconscious is always listening. In order to ensure the effectiveness of the affirmations, they have to be repeated with strong conviction, desire, and passion – even if you struggle to believe them in the beginning.

Using positive affirmations for just a few minutes every day and then continuing to repeat negative statements day in and day out will create undesirable results. Words and statements work both ways, either building or destroying.

Your words and thoughts reflect your inner goals, so modify them when necessary to reach your desired outcome.

"Most folks are about as happy as they want to be." - Abraham Lincoln

---

If you're like most people, you probably repeat negative statements in your mind without even knowing you're doing it. Do you keep telling yourself that you cannot do something, you're too lazy, you're not smart enough, you're not good enough, you can't afford it, you can't succeed, or that you're going to fail? Your subconscious accepts these statements as true and attracts corresponding events and situations to substantiate those statements.

Begin to reprogram your thought processes and create new habits. It's similar to building a muscle. Consistency and repetition is essential. Using positive thinking techniques, visualizations, and positive affirmations, it is possible to achieve whatever you want. At a personal level, it will transform your life, your health, and renew your joy and passion for life.

Business people use these techniques to develop personal power or gain a competitive edge.

Use only positive words, describing what you really want. If you desire to lose weight, don't say, "I'm not fat" or "I'm losing weight." Those are negative statements, bringing into the mind mental images of what you do *not* want. Instead, say, "I'm my ideal weight" or "I'm healthy and happy." Such phrases evoke positive images in the mind of what you want, referring to your goals as if they have already occurred. This keeps your mind focused on what you *do* want.

Always affirm in the present tense, not the future tense. Saying, "I will be rich" means that you intend to be rich one day, but you'll never get there because you'll always be affirming a future that never comes. It's more effective to say and feel, "I'm rich" or "Money flows to me effortlessly." Your subconscious mind will then work overtime to make this happen in the present.

The power of affirmations can help you transform your life. By stating what you want to be true in your life, you mentally and emotionally see and feel it as true, regardless of your current circumstances, and thereby attract it into your life.

It isn't enough to stop the negative thinking. You need to replace it with something more empowering. Erase the old tapes in your head, and create new ones. Imagine waking up each morning bursting with excitement, full of energy and happiness for the new day! It really is possible!

Why Positive Affirmations Work

Affirmations program the mind in the same way that commands and code program a computer. The repeated words help you to focus your mind on your goal and automatically build corresponding mental images in your subconscious mind. The conscious mind, which is where your thoughts reside, starts this process, and the subconscious mind takes charge. By using this process consciously and intently, you can affect your subconscious mind, and thereby transform your habits, behaviors, mental attitude, and reactions. You can even reshape your entire life.

If you find yourself experiencing serious resistance or have identified an area of trauma in your life, I strongly urge you to seek professional support. The journey you are embarking on will release you from the past, but having proper support around you as you go through the process will make it so much easier.

Stay away from Toxic Words and Emotions. Stay Positive!

"I CHOOSE to make the REST of my Life the BEST of my Life."
– Louise Hay

Action Steps

Ask yourself:

✓ What toxic words do I use in my vocabulary that do not serve me?

✓ What are some positive things I can say about myself today?

Chapter 6

Secret #4: Breaking the Trance

Break the trance of denial, and acknowledge your bad habits.

Habits are automatic responses that we continue because they help us feel better in the moment, regardless of any long-term benefit. These habits consist of behaviors, thoughts, emotions, and physical responses.

There are good habits and bad habits, of course. The bad habits cause immediate benefits, but they cause long-term harm. A bad habit would be eating chocolate cake because it looks good, tastes good, and feels good to eat. Before you know it, you start to justify how it is not so bad, after all it has eggs in it and that is a good source of protein and the dark chocolate is great for elevating your mood and has other health benefits, although they all vanish after adding sugar to it, but you believe it is going to make you feel good now. So before you know it, you find yourself with a second serving. You have the immediate benefit, but over time you start gaining an extra 5, 10, 20 or 50 pounds. Even worse you run the risk of diabetes or heart disease and over the long term it becomes a really bad habit.

An emotional bad habit might be anger. You might get others to leave you alone, but the long-term harm could be a heart attack or stroke from the stress.

These habits help you *"feel better"* immediately but long-term repetition is harmful. We give in to the **immediate relief or reward, and we pretend that life**

gets better when you perform these habits. At least that's what we think at the moment.

Good habits cause immediate long-term benefits. Believe it or not, every single person from infancy was taught good habits. We were taught how to eat healthy. We were taught to exercise as kids. At least when I was younger, we ran around a lot. We didn't sit in front of the computer or television all day. We were taught that there are certain things that are good for us and things that are bad for us. We were taught not to smoke or do drugs, for example.

A lot of the time, our habits don't align with our core values and beliefs. Maybe you value good health, but you have the habit of smoking. If you value good health and decide to take a walk rather than sit in front of the TV, that would be a habit in alignment with your values and beliefs.

Many of our bad habits get started as a result of stress. This is when we seek that immediate reward. We're just looking for a way to *"feel better"* as soon as possible. It's scientifically proven that the unconscious mind takes over in these moments and actually controls us.

The mind thinks in ten-minute increments. So, if you have a bad habit, your mind evaluates it for the next ten minutes. It doesn't think about the long-term unless you consciously make the choice to think that way.

How do you break the trance? Besides becoming aware of your habits, pay attention to the triggers that put you in the trance that leads to the bad habit. These triggers can be stinkin thinkin, phobias, stress, depression, panic attacks, neuroses, frustration, headaches, or many other possibilities.

It is important to understand that many illnesses are caused by what we do to ourselves. It's 90% environmental, which includes food and our thoughts. So what you think is important.

Neuro is referring to your neurological processes or your thinking; the way you use your thoughts and senses to understand what is happening around you.

Linguistics consists of your words, the way you use language, and how it influences you and others. Tonality and emphasis can alter the meaning of words, too. If I say, "This is good for you," just emphasizing the word GOOD can change the entire meaning. If I say, "Don't be bad," I can say it in a sexual way or a judgmental way or a comic way.

Begin to notice not just what you say to yourself, but also how you say it.

Time to break the trance: you get to choose to change the channel and the program you are running. You have been **programming** your behaviors through your experiences. You have organized ideas and actions, which produced expected and unexpected results to help you achieve specific goals in your life. For example, you already know if you eat chocolate cake you're going to feel better. It's an expected result.

Stop Being Scared to Make a Mistake

Peer pressure doesn't stop in high school. We're still afraid of making a mistake and being judged by others. Some of our bad habits are a result of following the crowd — eating, drinking, and smoking especially fall into this category. But if your friends complain a lot, you may feel you have to do it, too, even though it causes negative results in your life.

Ask yourself better questions about what will bring you happiness. Start internally, it is an inside job.

Action Steps

✓ *Write a list of bad habits you follow to "feel better" that are not aligned with your core values or beliefs.*

✓ *Create a list of good habits you can adopt that would make you "feel better" in the long term.*

✓ *What are some good habits you can exercise in replace of the bad to get more of what you want?*

Chapter 7

Secret #5: Uncovering Unconscious Patterns of Behavior

Have you heard the expression, it is only the tip of the iceberg? Ever wonder what that really meant? **Freud's Iceberg Model for Conscious, Preconscious and Unconscious** is a great metaphor. Only 10% of an iceberg is visible (**conscious**), while the other 90% is beneath the water (**preconscious and unconscious**).

The **Preconscious** is allotted approximately 10-15%, and the **Unconscious** is allotted an overwhelming 75-80%. Our external behaviors – what we do – are all affected by the **Conscious** mind.

The preconscious mind is the *"why"* we do what we do – our motivation.

Conscious mental activity is intelligent, analytical, conceptualizing, and logical with a narrow focus on everyday events. Unconscious processes are emotion-based, intuitive, and fantasy-prone – a non-judgmental repository of accumulated knowledge and experience, or your identity deep down. Approximately 90% of our mental activity is unconscious. The conscious mind allows us to rationalize what we do and helps us reduce our anxiety in this way, and the unconscious mind functions automatically, keeping our autonomous system going without our conscious attention.

We tend to act out whatever our unconscious mind tells

us. It basically does what it's programmed to do, so if it has come to believe negative things, it will sabotage our lives.

Your conscious mind is the seat of your will power and motivation. It is your external guide to what you do. Your unconscious mind, or internal guide to why you do it, is where your beliefs and values reside. If the conscious mind and the unconscious mind are not in harmony, the unconscious mind always wins in the end. This is why it can be so hard to make lasting changes through "*will power*" alone.

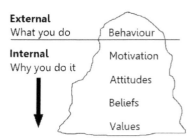

The good news is that with **Neuro Linguistic Programming (NLP)**, you can easily access the unconscious mind, address distorted or outdated beliefs, create a new self-image, and make lasting changes. In many ways, it is true that it's all in the (unconscious) mind.

To manifest something in the outside world, it helps to establish a good mental picture first. Imagination is key.

So, sometimes you might be motivated to do something, and you don't even know why you're doing it. I was motivated to be successful. I didn't know why I was motivated at the time, except that my parents told me in order to be successful, I had to make a certain amount of money and do specific things. Therefore, my preconscious was motivated and helped drive me toward success.

Your conscience controls the actions you take and your external behavior. But the "why" you do something, as well as the attitudes, beliefs, and values behind your actions, were instilled in your preconscious and unconscious mind.

People often say that in order to get to the unconscious, you need a psychoanalyst or psychologist. But as a **Licensed Master NLP Practitioner**, I can attest that you're able to access your unconscious yourself. I teach people these skills every day.

You have already learned some strategies in this book to understand your subconscious mind. Once you apply them, it can take your life to a new level.

To understand your behavior, you need to determine the reason behind it. There are two possible reasons: Are you doing something to avoid pain or gain pleasure?

If you're doing something to avoid pain, you may not eat vegetables, for example, because you perceive it as more painful than eating cake. Or you think exercise is painful, so you avoid it. Your thought process might go something like this, "I really need to exercise, but I have to get my gym bag and put all my stuff in it. I have to find my gym clothes and go to the gym. When I get there, I have to deal with a locker. Then, there's all this equipment, there are sweaty people, I'm going to sweat, and I have to take a shower there. Then, I have to do my hair and get ready to leave." You make it such a big deal in your head that it sounds painful to even think about it, let alone do it.

Like the above, we sometimes associate actions with pain just because it's the story we've told ourselves. We'll do more to avoid pain than we will do to gain pleasure.

If you change your thinking, your story can be that you'll get pleasure from going to the gym for an hour because you'll have more energy and endorphins, you'll feel better, you'll end up looking the way you want to look, you'll get the attention you want from your significant other, you'll meet people, and you'll feel healthier.

Understand your patterns of behavior and what defines your values, beliefs, and attitudes.

Action Steps

✓ What are some things you say you want to do but don't do?

✓ What is your story associated with these actions that you want to do but don't do?

✓ Are you working to avoid pain, or are you working toward pleasure?

✓ How can you change your story to make a good habit something you will love to do?

✓ What benefits will this new habit give you when you adopt it?

Chapter 8

Secret #6: Stop Waiting for Perfection

Stop waiting for perfection, and eliminate the excuses that are keeping you stuck. Shame, guilt, frustration, depression, feeling sorry for yourself, making things bigger than they are, blaming others for your troubles and procrastination are all excuses that keep you from moving forward. There is never going to be a perfect time or condition when everything goes the way you want it. So, being ambitious is great, but aiming for perfection is unrealistic. It's impractical and debilitating.

Tony Robbins once told me, **"Perfection is the lowest standard."** When I first heard that, I was insulted. I was a perfectionist at that time, but once I understood it better, I was relieved because his statement took the pressure off. I made a decision that day to **strive for imperfection,** and I have been doing that for the last 20 years. After all, the word imperfect is really **"I'm Perfect."**

The trick is to simply aim for consistent improvement – consciously, methodically working toward just becoming better than before. As long as you are taking **imperfect action,** you are making progress.

"If you wait for perfect conditions, you'll never get anything done." – Ecclesiastes 11:4-5

Trying to Be Perfect Can Be Painful

After years of chasing perfection, I wondered why I was never able to catch it. I spent most of my life letting it rule me. It set the standard for everything that followed. It validated me when I did well and scrutinized me when I didn't.

I decided to look up the definition and see why I was never able to attain it. There was no room for error. This meant that I was never good enough and always striving for more. I had to be superlative, above the rest, the best. It was hard to attain that standard all the time and often left me feeling like a failure. I would then punish myself for not achieving my goals, and I sacrificed a lot over the years trying to live up to this "perfect" image – something that I couldn't see, hear, or feel. I was relentless and ambitious; doing whatever it took but seldom achieved what they called "perfect." What about you?

Well, you can imagine my excitement when I opened the dictionary and learned we have all defined perfection imperfectly for years. See for yourself:

Definition of Perfect...*per·fect*/ˈpərfikt/
according to Google...

"Having all the required or desirable elements, qualities, or characteristics; as good as it is possible to be."

Even the word PERFECT doesn't expect perfection as many of us defined it!

Perfection is, broadly, a state of completeness and flawlessness. http://en.wikipedia.org/wiki/Perfect

The word "perfection" derives from the Latin "*perfectio*", and "perfect" — from "*perfectus*." These expressions in turn come from "*perficio*" — "to finish", "to bring to an end." "*Perfectio*(n)" thus literally means "a finishing", and "perfect*(us)*" — "finished", much as in grammatical parlance ("perfect").

The ethical question of perfection concerns not whether man *is* perfect, but whether he *should* be. And if he *should* be, then how is this to be attained?

"Do your best, forget the test!" – Deb Battersby

Upgrade Your Video Player

As I mentioned before, you have to change the tape in your head, and that includes the video – the pictures you play in your mind because they are part of the story you tell yourself. And most of those stories aren't true.

So, put in a new DVD, and reprogram your mind for a happy and healthy future. If you're waiting for those perfect conditions, they will never come.

Avoid focusing on what you cannot do. Instead, focus on what you can do and accomplish without expecting approval and recognition from others. Accept yourself as you are right now.

Welcome imperfections by focusing on what you have gained from the process of doing the best you can.

Allow yourself to make mistakes, and forgive yourself for them. Failure is a necessary part of learning.

Today, every time I make what others would call a mistake, I celebrate. It's funny to see how others react to this. I mentor a group of women, and we have a weekly call together. The first week, we had challenges with the phone line. When we finally all connected, I celebrated and shouted, "We did it! YEAH!!!" As you can imagine, they thought I was crazy.

Then, we had challenges with the members getting locked out of the website. As some members became frustrated, I relieved their frustration by asking, "Where else does this happen in your life?" That became a phenomenal call for everyone. Change the meaning, and change your life!!! Go out and make mistakes. It means you're living a full life.

Focus on What's Right

Whatever we focus on grows bigger – so big, in fact, that it can block the view of everything else. We can turn nothing into something and create a huge problem when the situation is actually small if viewed from the perspective of our strengths.

Too often, we spend time focusing on what's wrong when we can be searching for what's right. Finding what's wrong is easy, but to be able to see the bright side is true power. Learning to turn challenges into opportunities is freeing. When you can call upon your strengths, not your weaknesses, to do what you do best, you function at a higher level. You will build more confidence in yourself and have the ability to continually climb even higher.

Over the years trying so hard to be perfect, I conditioned myself to see what was wrong with situations and aimed at always making them better. The obstacle arrived when I was no longer able to see what was right. I was so critical and looking for the bad that I missed the good. I can remember several occasions where I would beat myself up over what I did wrong and negate all that I did right. Do you know anyone like that?

I once spoke at a seminar before thousands of people. I prepared for days, rehearsing the entire speech in my head dozens of times. I did an outstanding job and even got a standing ovation. It was incredible, but the demonstration with the audience took more time than I expected, leaving me feeling rushed at the end. I felt I didn't do as good a job as I could have if I had planned the time better. I became disappointed in myself and wouldn't let it go. All I could focus on was what I had done "wrong." Later, people congratulated me for a job well done, and all I could think of was how I messed up.

This practice of looking for what is wrong was not serving me; it was causing me much pain and dripped into so many areas of my life. I decided to adopt a new attitude and belief, looking for what was right. Instead of noticing what was unsatisfactory, inaccurate, astray, defective, bad, or who was at fault, I looked for what was satisfactory, accurate, good, and right.

I adopted a new question "What's good about this?"

I changed my story from how I didn't manage my time to how great the demonstration worked and the awesome job I did getting the point across to the audience. Can you see how this would be more empowering and productive than the former attitude?

Knowing What to Focus On

So often we try to be good at everything to prove our super powers, when that effort actually leaves us feeling powerless. As Deepak Chopra said, "There is something that you can do better than anyone else in the whole world." It's your job to find out what that is and do it. Focus on what you do best, and chances are, it's also what you love to do the most. Whatever you focus on grows.

Think about it this way: On a scale of 1-10, we need more 10's in the world. A person doing what he/she loves and does well eliminates mediocrity. For example, when it comes to administrative work and numbers, I'm average, a 5 at best, spending more time to get better at it will only make me perhaps a 7. As a public speaker, I'm perhaps a 9. So, if I invest my time and effort in this ability, I might be able to attain a level 10.

I also don't enjoy dealing with numbers, charts, and figures, so it isn't the best use of my time. Spending more time with activities you want to improve but don't love will only take time away from activities you do enjoy. In other words, you are stealing time from the 10's in your life just to bring a 2 up to a mediocre 4.

Too often, we focus on what we do not do well; feeling frustrated and angry about it and thinking there's something wrong with us.

Years back, when I was building one of my businesses, I found that there were certain jobs I was excited about doing and did extremely well. I loved helping people, being creative and speaking but would get baffled when confronted with administration, tedious tasks and small minds. My whole attitude would shift. My attention was getting caught up with the wrong things and not enough of the right. I was trying to do everything and found myself at times doing nothing. It cost me time and money. The time I lost procrastinating took far longer than what was required for the task.

The solution was learning to delegate. This presented new challenges. I didn't want to let go of the controls. I couldn't justify paying others for what I could do myself. Then, my friend, Elizabeth Weber, said, "Hire someone to do that. You make more money doing what you do best than what it costs you to have someone else do it." She was right. I made more money doing what I loved than I could if I continued to do the tasks I hated.

Today, I'm no longer the martyr who has to do it all herself. I have taken off my superwoman costume.

"According to this law [the law of Dharma], you have a unique talent and a unique way of expressing it. There is something that you can do better than anyone else in the whole world – and for every unique talent and unique expression of that talent, there are also unique needs. When these needs are matched with the creative expression of your talent, that is the spark that creates affluence. Expressing your talents to fulfill needs creates unlimited wealth and abundance."- Deepak Chopra

---

Watch What You Put In

Feed your mind with good thoughts and positive affirmations, and feed your body with healthy food choices, not with comfort or convenience foods. You are special, so treat yourself that way.

Food has a huge effect on your mind. It affects your endorphin levels, for example. Endorphins are produced in the body, and they bind the neuroreceptors in the brain and act on the central and peripheral nervous system to alleviate pain. A lot of health challenges can be attributed to the foods we put into our bodies and the thoughts we put into our minds.

Remember to H.A.L.T.: Hungry, Angry, Lonely, Tired = HALT.
Stop what you are doing. Eat only when your body is hungry, and rest when you're tired and reacting to something.

Hungry

Angry

Lonely

Tired

"I Want to Feel Better Now"

When you feel shame, guilt, frustration, or depression, do you sabotage yourself with comfort or convenience foods? If so, you're not alone. All your mind knows is: **"I want to feel better now."** Remember: If it's a behavior that won't serve you long-term, it's probably a bad habit. Treat yourself to things that will be healthy and will serve you better. Create a more fulfilling today and move toward a vision, purpose, or mission.

Start thinking outside yourself, and find a mission or a purpose that will fill you with passion and drive you. When you think of others, there is no time to think about yourself. You will find most of your problems will disappear. Have you ever noticed that when you're doing something you love with people you care about, the time flies? It's when we have downtime to sit and ponder that we sabotage ourselves. It's highly unlikely that you will ever feel depressed if you don't focus so much on yourself.

The challenge most people confront is that when they are trying to overcome something, they feel they have to give it up. This leads to deprivation. You feel like you're missing out on that chocolate cake you want so much. It makes you think of cake all the time. (I'm sorry; now, I have you thinking about chocolate cake. Let's think about apples instead!)

I just used food as an example because it's an easy one for me. It's like the old adage, "Don't think about the pink elephant." You can't do it, right? It's because your mind doesn't hear the word DON'T!

Instead, say, "Don't think about how I can make today even better." Or set a goal to meet more people. If you find something to replace that thing you want that's bad for you – something that is more aligned with your values and beliefs – you won't concentrate on what you don't have. You will be headed in the direction of what you want and you will have no time to sabotage yourself.

The challenge is that most people don't have a purpose. Much of their life is spent doubting their beliefs and believing their doubts, wasting their moments and seeing no future. So, when they aim, they have no target. Of course, that means they always miss, only to get caught up later on in stinkin thinkin.

Have you ever found yourself in front of a TV or on Facebook, saying, "I'm only going to watch for five minutes" Then, hours go by, and the whole evening is gone? Facebook is a poor replacement for love and connection that you will never get through a computer. It's static. Make sure you get out and spend actual quality time with people, doing things that are fulfilling to you. That's living.

Change your stories, change your life!

Action Steps

✓ Write down all the areas in your life in which perfection has been your enemy.

✓ What has being perfect prevented you from doing?

✓ What can you delegate that would help you feel better?

✓ Where do you excel and want to achieve more?

✓ How can you make a difference in the world with your gifts?

Chapter 9

Secret #7: Making Peace, Practicing Gratitude, and Celebrating!

Lasting change comes with changing your identity. If you were a smoker, and you now say, "I'm a non-smoker," that's very different from saying, "I stopped smoking on April 30th, and I'm counting the days." When you are still counting the days, you're focused on what was causing the temptation versus who you are. These words make a big difference in your body and will affect how you feel.

The strongest force in the human psyche is the need to stay consistent with your own identity. Decide what you want to create. What affirmations and convictions do you want to embody and keep at the deepest level?

The power of your beliefs and suggestions is remarkable. Your very life is your thinking and the results of your thinking processes. Claude M. Bristol said **"The secret of success lies not without, but within, the thoughts of man."** Your thoughts control every action.

"What you believe yourself to be, you are."

Practicing Gratitude

When you believe you already have what you want, you will start living a more fulfilling life. Count your blessings now, not later. Living in gratitude makes life so much easier. Sometimes you don't have much and aren't sure what to be grateful for. I remember somebody once say that "Everyday above ground is a good day." Well, I think that person has a very easy time thinking of what to be grateful for. When you open your eyes in the morning, that's something right there. Unfortunately, some people feel that gratitude is only merited when they achieve a specific result. When I make "X" amount of money or when this happens, then I will be grateful.

There is always something for which
to be thankful.

Remember: When your expectations are based on things you have no control over, you'll never be happy. So, make peace with any of the challenges you have had in your life. I know there are a lot of injustices out there. As you know, painful things have happened to me, too, but I choose not to focus my thinking there. I have decided that my past was a gift. It's responsible for making me stronger. It has made me who I am and what I have become. So I'm grateful for everything that has ever happened for me. At the time, it might not have felt good, but today, I'm grateful and wouldn't trade my life with anybody else's.

I have learned more lessons through those so-called negative experiences than anybody could have ever taught me in school. I had a hard time finding the gratitude when I was in the throes of all of it. So, in the beginning, I simply said, "I am grateful." Then, I said, "I have two hands, two feet, two eyes that can see, I can speak, and I can think."

Be grateful for everything you have. Be grateful that you were born in a country where you have democracy and the right to do what you want. You have no idea how privileged we are until you leave the USA. My husband

and I traveled around the world this year and saw people not nearly as fortunate as we are. We have a roof over our head and a mattress to sleep on. These things are unheard of in some parts of the world. So, be grateful, and celebrate everything. Celebrate the smallest thing you have. There is no big victory that hasn't come from small wins that you might not notice if you wait. People wait until they get a promotion and feel only then that they've achieved something. Instead, celebrate just having a job! Celebrate having a day! Celebrate being in someone else's presence!

How does this apply to weight loss? If you want to lose weight, don't make the goal too big. If you do, you'll have to wait too long to celebrate. If you want to lose 50 pounds, celebrate every day that you don't put things in your body that would hurt you. That's a reason for celebration. You can build on that alone every day, and it will help you reach your ultimate goal.

Practice gratitude, and learn to love yourself for who you are rather than the person you think you should be. Be willing to leave the past behind you, and stop beating yourself up over things that were out of your control. Learn to be grateful and appreciate all that you have now versus waiting to have the perfect life. Stop comparing yourself to others to fit a mold that does not exist, and start to be *the Best "You" that You Can Be*!

Practice an *Attitude of Gratitude*.

"Every person is the creation of himself, the image of his own thinking and believing. As individuals think and believe, so they are." - Claude M. Bristol

---

93

Action Steps

✓ What new opportunities would you like to pursue this year?

✓ What exciting changes are you ready to make?

✓ How will you make the journey fun and inspiring?

✓ What one, helpful habit are you willing to develop to support your efforts?

"You're stronger than you think you are..."
- Winnie the Pooh

Chapter 10

20 Ways to Become FAB

"We are what our thoughts have made us; so take care about what you think. Words are secondary. Thoughts live; they travel far."

– Swami Vivekananda

When you stop chasing the wrong things, you give the right things a chance to catch you.

Here are some suggestions to get you started:

1. **Release the past** – Stay present, for you cannot change what happened but you can design what's next.

2. **Appreciate your mistakes** – You may have made some poor choices or loved the wrong people, but one thing's for sure: Mistakes mean you took action. They help you find more of what is right for you. Remember that you are not your mistakes; they are what you did, not who you are. Everything you did in your life prepared you for this moment and the moments that are yet to come.

3. **Spend time with people who make you happy** – Life is too short to spend time with people who drain the happiness out of you. Remember, it's not the people who stand by your side when you're at your best, but the ones who stand beside you when you're not. They are your true friends.

4. **Change your problems to challenges** – Look at problems as challenges you are going to conquer and solve, not challenges that will take you over. Become resourceful and search for the solutions or opportunities in everything that comes your way. Ask yourself better questions: "What's good about this?" has gotten me through many challenging times.

5. **Be honest with yourself** – You can lie to others, but "to thine own self be true," as William Shakespeare wrote. Only when we are honest with ourselves can we live congruent with whom we are. Then, you can live an authentic life.

6. **Put your needs first** – Losing yourself in the process of loving someone more than you love yourself and forgetting that you, too, are special is very painful and lonely. Yes, help others; but help yourself first. If you are not whole, there is nothing to offer anyone else, so "take care of your mothers' daughter."

"I believe that one defines oneself by reinvention. To not be like your parents. To not be like your friends. To be yourself. To cut yourself out of a stone."
–Henry Rollins

---

7. **Be yourself** – One of the greatest difficulties in being yourself is living in a world where everyone is trying to be like everyone else. The truth is someone will always be prettier, smarter, younger, but they will never be you. It is not about changing so that people will like you. Be yourself so that the right people will love you. You were born to be

outstanding, so "stand out." You are an original, so be the best you that you can be.

3. **Take imperfect action** – Doing something is so much better than doing nothing. Everyday success is achieved by doing it imperfectly. Each success has some form of failure before it. Most people end up regretting the things they did NOT do far more than the things they did. So just do it!

9. **Be happy with you first** – If you're not happy with who you are on the inside, you won't be happy in a long-term relationship with anyone else. You have to create stability within yourself before you can expect it from others. Many people look to others to make themselves feel better. You need to be happy with you first before you can really help others.

10. **The past does not equal the future** – If you were in a bad relationship, it doesn't mean all relationships are bad. Just because you had spinach once and didn't like the taste doesn't mean all spinach is bad. You might have had it prepared poorly and missed out on its wonderful flavor. Judging people, relationships, or circumstances based on what happened in the past will only hurt the new relationships and people and cause more misfortunes.

"Nobody can go back and start a new beginning, but anyone can start today and make a new ending."
– Maria Robinson

---

11. **Spend time in your own garden** – Your mind is a garden. Your thoughts are seeds. You can either grow flowers or weeds. Success is a battle between YOU and YOURSELF only. While you are comparing what other people are planting in their gardens, there may be weeds forming in yours. Weed your own garden, and concentrate on being better daily for you.

12. **Change the record** – If you are lucky enough to live a full life, there will be many challenges thrown your way. You can choose to focus on what is good in your life and get more of it, or you can lament over what is wrong and be miserable. When people ask how you are doing, say "Great!" "Awesome!" or "Wonderful!" Refrain from telling your story of despair unless you want more of the same. This practice will lead you to a better place, person, state of mind, or situation. Smile! Let everyone know that today you are a lot stronger than you were yesterday, and you will be.

13. **Forgive and let go** – Hate only hurts the person carrying it. Let go, or you will end up hurting yourself more. Forgiveness doesn't mean, "What you did to me is okay." It means, "I'm not going to carry this anger and hatred with me any longer, and it's time to move on." Forgiveness is the answer. Let go and find peace! Forgiveness when granted to others becomes a gift to you. Forgiveness given to yourself is liberating!

"Forgiveness is the fragrance that the violet sheds on the heel that has crushed it."
–Mark Twain

---

14. **You need never explain yourself** – Your friends don't need it, and your enemies won't believe it anyway. Just do what you know in your heart is right.

15. **Appreciate everything** – Enjoy the little things because one day you may look back and discover they were the big things. The best portion of your life will be the small, nameless moments you spend smiling with someone who matters most to you.

16. **Take responsibility for where you are now** – The extent to which you can achieve your dreams depends on the extent to which you take responsibility for your life. Your decisions and choices up to that moment lead you to where you are. When you blame others for what you're going through, you deny responsibility – you give others power over that part of your life.

17. **Be everything to you, not everything to everybody** – Trying to please everyone is impossible and will only leave you in despair. Being all you can be for you will be enough for that lucky person who graces your presence. So narrow your focus.

"You alone are ENOUGH.
You have nothing to prove to anybody."
–Maya Angelou

---

18. **Laugh more and worry less** – Worrying will not strip tomorrow of its burdens; it will strip today of its joy. Most of the things we worry about never happen, and they certainly do not happen the way we

finetofab

thought they would. So, laugh more and worry less. It will add years to your life.

19. **Focus on what you want** – Positive thinking is the secret of every great success story. If you awake every morning with the thought that something wonderful will happen in your life today, and you pay close attention, you'll often find that you're right.

20. **Be grateful** – Maintain an attitude of gratitude. No matter how good or bad you have it, wake up each day thankful for your life. Someone else is desperately fighting for theirs, and there is always someone else who has it worse than you. Instead of thinking about what you're missing, appreciate what you have. Remember that every day above ground is a good day.

"Develop an attitude of gratitude, and give thanks for everything that happens to you, knowing that every step forward is a step toward achieving something bigger and better than your current situation."
–Brian Tracy

About The Author

Lisa is the leading expert in empowering professionals to embrace inner peace and power in their lives, bringing them from feeling **fine** to being **FAB**. As a

Licensed Master NLP Master Practitioner, she works with leaders in all professions to break through barriers that "weigh them down." Lisa's tools improve relationships, family, business and financial futures leading to more authentic, fulfilling, and purposeful lives.

Lisa is #1 International Best-Selling Author. She was the guest host on the television show, *For The Health of It* with Dr. Barrett. She is a professional speaker who has trained more than 70,000 entrepreneurs in the last 20 years on wellness, leadership, and sales/marketing strategies to grow their businesses and their minds.

In 2011, Lisa became part of an elite group of Platinum Partners with Anthony Robbins and was personally coached by him. She met with master teachers from around the world while traveling to some of the most spectacular destinations on earth. She studied with some of the World's Leading Personal Growth Experts, Renowned Wellness Doctors, Psychologists, Neuro-Linguistic Programming (NLP) Masters and Creators, Non-Medical Alternative Guru's and Leaders spanning eight countries and eight states, flying over 100,000 miles. Certified as a Master NLP Practitioner.

In 2012, she was mentored and Licensed as a Master NLP Practitioner by the Co-Creator of NLP, Dr. Richard Bandler.

Lisa's powerful messages are delivered through books and webinars, as well as through her informative seminars. She writes, teaches, and lectures on the relationship between food, spending, spirituality, body and mind, and self.

With over 30 years of personal experience and education in every weight loss diet, Lisa has consulted with experts in the field, participated in personal development programs, and sought therapeutic remedies. Finally, she decided, "It's really not about the food." As a result, Lisa has been free from depression, disordered and compulsive eating, binge eating, and self-sabotage for decades and now is the Founder & CEO of fine to FAB.

Fine to FAB came about because of a need to create awareness and empower women that need more than a diet or a pill to make them feel better. The suffering and pain stems from years of conditioning that needs to be interrupted and replaced. With advertisements telling us how we should look and what to nip and tuck, it is no wonder so many women have poor self-esteem and body image. She believes, "If it were only about the diet, we would all be thin."

Lisa's message is: **"You are already Fabulous, Awesome & Beautiful – F.A.B.!"**

Mission: Create a movement to empower today's women to reclaim their peace & power now!

Limited Offer

fine
f^{to}ab

*Limited Offer: Request a
FREE Consultation

Lisa Lieberman-Wang and *fine* to fab invite you or one family member to a private consultation.

To register go to
www.*fine*tofab.com/freeconsult

If you have no access to a computer,
Call 1-877-250-7275*

Use Reference #_____

(If you were not given a Reference #, use your book receipt # or special promo code.)

Special Bonus Offer

Limited to those who are seriously being challenged and have tried many things but are still having a hard time overcoming them. It is time to get help. I have been there before and learned all the necessary tools to take back control and live a healthy and free life.

I'm working privately with a small group of women who are committed to eliminating their debilitating feelings about life, their looks, and food. This is for people who have "thought" themselves into stagnation, frustration, exhaustion, anxiety, depression, and even illness. If you feel as if you have alienated yourself from your family and friends, and you look to food for comfort or feel truly sick and tired of hurting yourself, I can help. (I find that it is usually smart and successful people who have the hardest time letting go and being nice to themselves.)

Request a FREE Consultation Now!

If you are serious, simply fill out the form, and request a free consultation now at:

www.finetofab.com/freeconsult

You may have been self-destructive for a long time, but it's time you change. It's time to give yourself more of what you deserve and live a healthy, great, authentic life.

We find people get this far and drop the ball … 90% will never follow through. So, if you are interested, fill out the request <u>right now</u>, and give me as much information as you can.

I'm only offering this to a limited few who qualify. So, if you are serious about making a change, tired of self-sabotage, mental binges, looking for answers, thinking a pill is going to fix you or looking to food for comfort ... if you are looking to make things better, take action now. I look forward to hearing from you. This is something I usually charge for, and I am offering this as a one-time thing. I would love to be able to make a difference in your life and help you change to live the life you want.

Request a free consultation now:

www.finetofab.com/freeconsult

"God, grant me the serenity to accept the things I
cannot change,
The courage to change the things I can,
And the wisdom to know the difference."
- Reinhold Niebuhr

Stay Connected
1-877-250-7275

FREE Online Resources
to help you be
Fabulous, Awesome, Beautiful!

www.LisaLiebermanWang.com
www.finetofab.com

fine to FAB Blog

www.finetofab.com/blog

FREE Webinars

www.ItsAllAboutWoman.com
www.MyMentalDiet.com

Nutrition & Weight Loss

www.IsotonicVitaminStore.com
www.ItsReallyNotAboutTheFood.com

 **LisaLiebermanWang
finetofab**

 LiebermanWang

Lisa Lieberman-Wang's
Transformational Programs
The Keys to Take You from fine to FAB

I have decades of hands on experience of what keeps us stuck and how to get out. I can honestly attribute 100% of my success to:

1. Mastering Your Language and Thinking.

2. Understanding Your Emotions and Behaviors.

3. Learning, applying, practicing and refining these distinctions make all the difference.

These principles are the foundation for the fine to FAB Transformational Programs. In my experience personal development, who you are, how you think, what your beliefs are, what habits, characteristics and how confident you are with yourself directly affect both your success and happiness. I believe when you "take care of our mothers daughter "first", all else is possible.

I have taken my education of successes and mistakes and created a series of live seminars, programs and products designed to help you succeed more quickly and easily. They are the blueprint to help women entrepreneurs, coaches, business owners and self-employed professionals achieve more now. You will learn how to apply these principles to every aspect of your life to accelerate from fine to FAB.

Fine to FAB Transformational Program

The 10 week group program includes mentoring from me personally, weekly conference calls, personalized attention, membership website complete with audios, videos, pre-work, exercises, and group forum. In addition, private nutritional counseling from an expert and an optional 2-day weekend seminar. If you are struggling with food, emotional eating, depression, anxiety, stress, self esteem or personal trauma keeping you from fulfilling your goals this is for you. Designed to help you easily break through the barriers that weigh you down, learn and understand your behavior patterns and give you the tools and resources to eliminate disempowering habits to move forward immediately living a more authentic life that is healthy, happy and free.

Fine to FAB Membership Program

The 12 month membership program is a self-study course designed to help women identify what is working for them and what is not and how to create a new plan for themselves. The program is pre-recorded lessons from Lisa with exercises, videos and downloads to start their own journey to living the life you desire.

Fine to FAB Weight Loss & Weight Management Program

The 3 month program is based on changing your thinking from "live to eat, to eat to live." You will be learning new tools to stop the patterns that no longer serve you and replacing them with healthier options. Understanding why you are eating and the needs it is filling for you and simple ways to easily apply these strategies that will help you drop the weight. This is not a diet but a way of life that follows a low glycemic lifestyle for those looking to lose weight and/or a maintenance program.

FINE to FAB Private One-on-One Mentoring

For those individuals who require private one-on-one mentoring a customized program can be put together for you. I will work with you step-by-step to help you move to the next level of performance in your career and your life.

Working with a trusted mentor, you develop complete clarity about who you are, what you want, where you are going and it is the fastest way to achieve your goals.

Private mentoring takes on many forms, ranging from half to full days, to monthly or quarterly sessions spread out over 6-12 months. Having access to a mentor is an exceptionally powerful way to leverage your time and your results.

If you're done wasting time and money looking for a quick fix and going nowhere, if you know there is a gap in where you are and where you want to be and you are committed to doing what it takes to achieve the results you desire and deserve, if you are serious about reaching your full potential and breaking through as a fabulous, awesome, beautiful person, I want to encourage you to do what I have done:

1. Invest in yourself (which is the key to growth)

2. Learn the critical distinctions so you can create better choices (which is the key to a better life)

3. Do whatever it takes to create excellence, mastery and contribution (which is the key to fulfillment)

For more information on Transformational, Mentoring or Private Programs offered by me visit, www.LisaLiebermanWang.com. I want to encourage you to contact me either through email, my websites, or directly on the phone at 1-877-250-7275. If you are looking for answers, I can help.

Remember you are already Fabulous, Awesome and Beautiful!

Love,

Lisa

Lisa Lieberman-Wang

Praise for fine to FAB
Transformational Program

"To any woman (or man) that has ever questioned their life; fine to FAB is the awakening, awareness and emotional connector to empower you to address those questions with true answers, real (easy) change, and zero blame. It's a roadmap to success, discovery of where true love comes from, and the individual's toolbox to happiness in whatever challenge(s) you face or don't even know you have...THIS WORKS, people will wonder why you're smiling, constantly!"

-**Gayle Elder**, Former District Court Judge, Current Successful FAB Entrepreneur

"Carrying your past around with you in the form of extra weight? Were you once an outgoing, successful, fun loving person? Then, after some bumps in the road now find yourself sinking deeper and deeper down a hole, only to bury yourself with food. With Lisa's help and the "fine to FAB" program it is possible to stop this pattern and free yourself from your past and the food. Once you start to go through the process you'll find that all aspects of your life will improve, and not just your waistline."

-**Anne-Marie Gunthrie**, Education Specialist

"From an early age, I began searching for "more" I always knew I wanted "more" but I wasn't sure what "more" was, or how to achieve it! I learned more about myself and my path spending an hour with Lisa than I did spending over 2 years with a therapist. Lisa's program was not only an eye and heart-opener, but the best word I can use to describe it is a metamorphosis. I went into the program feeling like a straggly caterpillar and came out realizing what an amazing butterfly I have become! Stop settling for less and know you deserve the best!"

-**Sarah Dawe**, Project Manager

"This is Lisa D. Lieberman-Wang at her best as she takes you from where you are (fears and phobias) to where you want to be (strong and courageous). Let your transformational journey begin.... phenomenal!"

-**Diane Lane**, CNA

"I came to Lisa feeling "stuck" in a few areas of my life. I have been on a 20 year journey of healing and self-improvement, utilizing various conventional and non-conventional methods. I have stopped destructive eating, accomplished many goals and changed my thinking in many ways, yet I was still feeling stuck. The tools and guidance I received during Lisa's Fine to FAB class have transformed my life! My level of peace and contentment has multiplied. I have accomplished new goals and continue to move forward. I incorporate the tools I learned into my life daily and teach them to my clients, children and friends. Lisa's ultimate goal is to love yourself as you are and create the life you want to live."

-**Karen Kremzar**, Occupational Therapist, Health and Wellness Coach

"I have never felt so alive! Gaining clarity about my family & business goals has inspired me to take the actions I needed. Lisa's coaching style offers inspiration and guidance without judgment. This was pivotal in helping me discover exactly who I am. I use the term "coaching" freely because Lisa told me she never thinks of her work as "coaching". To me, Lisa's work is the definition of coaching: "Teaching or training process in which an individual gets support while learning to achieve a specific personal or professional result or goal". Lisa, YOU ARE A #1 COACH!"

-**Cindy Sheridan Murphy**, Personal Weight Mgmt, Health & Life Coach

"I believe that life is short and we were designed to live an extraordinary life, no matter how old we are. Lisa has given me tools to get "unstuck" in my old habits of processing my thoughts and not self sabotage myself. Thank you, Lisa, for helping me live my dash in a more productive and healthy way."

-**Pattie Scarce**, Entrepreneur

"I've gone to training after training in my life. I've been to therapy I've been to everything. And nothing has been able to get me past the blockages that have kept me from being as successful as I want to be. And I've lived in the past for the last 50 years. And when I heard about Lisa's class and I listened to her webinar I was just blown away by the things that she was saying that I had to do. So I recommend the program for anyone who has had things in their life that they haven't been able to get rid of and they couldn't get past. She knows how to help you get past that. It's just really awesome."

- **Pam Soliday**, Engineer

"One of the things that I have found in this course is understanding stories and how we live in them. It's really moved me into a place where I don't react based on my story but I respond based on the truth of what's going on in the situation. I've gained focus about where I want to go and how I want to get there. It's amazing. I would recommend this for anyone who is looking for a breakthrough. That's what I came to find was a breakthrough. And I think I've found that door opened where all I have to do is just walk through it and do the things that I have learned. I absolutely would recommend fine to FAB to any woman who is looking to be who she is supposed to be."

-Atha T White, ND MH CPT

"I have gone through the fine to FAB seminar, workshop, life changing experience. I came to it not being able to move. I am leaving with an action plan. I have things to do. I am doing things. It is designed for people who need to figure out what they want and how to get there. I recommend it for anyone who needs to examine their life, who they are, why they are and what they need to do.

Lisa I want to thank you from the bottom of my heart and grateful that you are in my life because what this has done for me is validate me, myself being a single woman with very few attachments, I still have a purpose in life now. Thank you."

-Cayte Thorpe, Singer

"Fine to FAB has given me a definite purpose as to what is most important to me, the ability to prioritize it and the tools to develop an action plan. I think anybody that is looking for what do I do now and needs help would benefit from working with Lisa. This is absolutely a program that you need to look at and invest in yourself. We take care of our family and our husbands and the people around us but the reality is if we don't work to take care of ourselves and do what's the best for us we can't do what's the best for somebody else. This is absolutely something that you need to look into so that you can be the best that you can be."

-Heidi Hartley, Teacher

"I did the fine to FAB program because while I was successful in some parts of my life but I realized I needed to grow and change. I had some issues from the past to deal with and they were getting in the way of what I wanted for the future. Unlike a lot of self-help stuff that I have been through before, Lisa didn't focus on the old stories she allowed me to get rid of them in my life, create new ones and see myself the way I am now. I would recommend this personally for anybody who wants to grow personally or lead others because it starts with you. This has been life changing. There's only so long that I can go on pretending that I believed I was good when I didn't. Now I know that I am a good person. It's something that I know would have developed into conflict. Today it's totally not something I have to worry about anymore. I would really recommend it for anybody who has had some issues about who they think they are."

- **Jessica Anderson**, Entrepreneur

Lisa you are brilliant! We miss so much of our lives picking on ourselves leading to self-sabotage, WOW! Now I know! What a different life I am living! Thank you! We women want to live and love, but somehow we mess ourselves up. The fog has lifted, I can see, feel, love and grow and can now pass it on to my children. You're the BEST!

- **Linda Trudden**, Goddess of Gilgo Beach

"Lisa is one of those ladies who has been thru the ringer and come up smelling like a ROSE. She has copulated all of her 30 plus years of learning into the fine to FAB Transformation education syllabus. After attending the fine to FAB Transformation program, my life will never be the same. My family, friends and colleagues will benefit for future generations as I share my new and updated knowledge to be FAB..."

-**Nellie Bell**, Real Estate Investor, Health & Wellness Coach

"Lisa Lieberman-Wang has touched my life in more ways than she knows. Her sincerity and her love to help others shine through the pages of this book as she does in her program. Feeling stuck in my life and feeling overwhelmed and overweight I was at a point where I even cried when I danced with abandon. Eventually Lisa guided me to a point where "life" became a dance of joy! I will be forever grateful for learning how to make decisions where I am the pilot of my life. I am indeed "taking care of my mother's daughter." Thank you Lisa. Bravo!!!"

-**Elizabeth L. Castro**, Teacher

Acknowledgements

I am grateful to be surrounded by such extraordinary friends, family, associates, mentors, coaches, world-renowned doctors, psychologists, licensed master NLP practitioners, creators, non-medical alternative gurus, leaders, and clients who have made a profound contribution to my life and life's purpose. This book and my work with fine to FAB stem largely from their influence and their belief in my mission to help women.

In particular, my deepest gratitude and love go to:

Yardley Wang, my husband and the wind beneath my wings, for being my best friend, believing in me and encouraging me to follow my heart. His support and vision made it possible for me to move forward with my mission and passion to help empower women.

My mother, who is the definition of unconditional love, for always being a raving fan and believing in everything I do. (I love you up to the sky...)

My dad, for wanting the best for me and teaching me so many valuable lessons over the years. Offering a different perspective and always being present for me in my life.

Bruce Lieberman, my brother, who has always been there for me, having all the answers and supporting me in my missions.

Howard Dail, a part of our family, another raving fan always supportive in every way. My Aunt Mary Ann Rosenberg, who has never failed to be there to lend a helping hand.

Loren Slocum, mentor, long-time friend and author, who told me two years ago in Egypt on a Tony Robbins Platinum Partner trip that I was supposed to do this. I fought with her, and look at me now. I love you for being persistent and knowing me as well as you do.

- Tony Robbins deserves significant credit for being my mentor and friend. Almost twenty years ago, he was the gentle giant who was tough and honest with me when I didn't want to hear it. Recently, he was there again for another critical point in my life when I vacillated on my decision to make my mission public with helping women with disordered eating, something I had only done privately for years.

- My story of becoming an expert began by learning from these incredible teachers in the months and years following my hospitalization at the age of eighteen: Mark Victor Hansen, Jack Canfield, Jim Rohn, Deepak Chopra, Earl Nightingale, Napoleon Hill, Anthony Robbins, Brian Tracy, Wayne Dyer, Tom Hopkins, Dale Carnegie, John Gray, Jay Abraham, Jack Canfield, Byron Katie, Andy Andrew, Dr. Donny Epstein, John Maxwell, Brian Klemmer, Joyce Meyer, Louise Hay, Eckhart Tolle, Dalai Lama, Paulo Coehlo, Stephen Covey, Zig Ziglar, Og Mandino, Dr. Donny Epstein, Guru Singh, Dr. Richard Bandler, Deb Battersby, Carol Swanson, Carolyn Sampson, Jeffrey Zavik, Stephan Stavrakis and other legends both living and past. I'm honored to count several of you as friends and peers. I am aware that I stand among greatness and will forever be grateful for your guidance.

- Linda Trudden, my best friend, for all the laughter and fun. My deepest appreciation for the countless hours she spent going over my speeches and seminars over the years.

- Elizabeth Weber, my lifelong friend and mentor, for her belief in me, which is what made it possible to earn millions. Supported me in finding my true purpose and as I continued my education, she told me "You should teach them." I took her advice. (You're the best, and I mean it!)

- J.R. Ridinger and Loren Ridinger for their vision hard work, and persistence of Shop.com powered by Market America, which has given me the financial independence to now fulfill my purpose.

Jacki Blasko, my dearest friend with the biggest heart, who saw this vision before I did. I thank her for praying for me and supporting me in my mission to help women.

Debi Waldeck, a friend and author of *Saving Generation Next*, for her incredible wisdom and knowledge of wellness and for her support.

Mary Allen, my soul buddy, friend and author, The Power of Inner Choice, for her vision and persistence, which has inspired me for the past 20 years. I thank her for being a powerful role model.

Kimberly Bonniksen, a friend, marketing genius and my editor, founder of The Legend People, for helping make "fine to FAB" legendary.

The Rotary Clubs, Knights of Columbus, Chamber of Commerce, ADP, Market America, Shop.com and more than 70,000 entrepreneurs in the last 20 years for allowing me to teach on personal development, wellness, leadership, and sales & marketing strategies to grow themselves, their businesses, and their minds.

I want to thank my business associates for making it possible to continue on with my purpose and life mission to help empower women to find peace and power in their lives.

My FAB Women who did the work and are now living examples. They are touching the lives of many and will change future generations to live an authentic life that is happy, healthy, and free. Together, we will touch more lives than Oprah.

Finally, I want to thank everyone who has helped me share my message — friends, family, and associates. Your support will help us create a movement to change the world, one person at a time. I love and appreciate you.

Footnotes

[1] Jill Bolte Taylor's stroke of insight
www.ted.com/talks/jill_bolte_taylor_s_powerful_stroke_of_insight.
html

[2] 2 Innate fears we were born with.
www.wiki.answers.com/Q/What_are_innate_human_fears

[3] *from Dale Carnegie literature
-secondary source: ResearchPoll.com

[4] UNC School of Medicine April 22, 2008 — Sixty-five percent of American women between the ages of 25 and 45 report having disordered eating behaviors, according to the results of a new survey by SELF Magazine in partnership with the University of North Carolina at Chapel Hill.
http://www.med.unc.edu/www/newsarchive/2008/april/survey-finds-disordered-eating-behaviors-among-three-out-of-four-american-women

[5] The Global Language Monitor

[6] www.slate.com/articles/life/the_good_word/2006/04/word_count.
html

[7] Jeanne McCarten Teaching Vocabulary, Lessons from the Corpus, Lessons for the Classroom.
English language has doubled in size in the last century, Richard Alleyne, Science Correspondent, *The Telegraph*, December 16, 2010

[8] Tony Robbins, Date With Destiny manual.
* Quote on Cover, Pictures on pg 8 & 12 are not endorsements from Tony Robbins

[9] Book by Sharon Begley, "Train Your Mind, Change Your Brain: How a New Science Reveals Our Extraordinary Potential to Transform Ourselves"

Lisa Lieberman-Wang
Speaker, Trainer, Seminar Leader

Lisa Lieberman-Wang is a top professional speaker who has addressed more than 70,000 people throughout the United States and Internationally.

Lisa's keynote speeches, talks, and seminars are described as "inspiring, entertaining, motivational and informative." She speaks on empowering women, self-help, personal growth and business development. Her audiences include companies, businesses, associations and charities.

Lisa will carefully customize her talk for your needs. For more information about booking Lisa, visit www.LisaLiebermanWang.com or call **1-877-250-7275** today.

You're FAB!
(Fabulous, Awesome, Beautiful)

Share this book with someone you love.
www.finetofabbook.com